LOYAL AND LETHAL
LADIES OF ESPIONAGE

LOYAL AND LETHAL
LADIES OF ESPIONAGE

———— ▼ ————

Tom Moon

iUniverse.com, Inc.
San Jose New York Lincoln Shanghai

Loyal and Lethal Ladies of Espionage

Published by iUniverse.com, Inc.

For information address:
iUniverse.com, Inc.
5220 S 16th, Ste. 200
Lincoln, NE 68512
www.iuniverse.com

ISBN: 0-595-14749-6

Printed in the United States of America

The 100+ women whose stories are told fit all of those classifications and add their own shadings of intrigue, revenge, cunning, craftiness, patriotism and bravery. From the earliest days of the Old Testament (Esther, Delilah, and Rahab) to today's women we see how they were led, what they did, how they did it and why.

Chinese Empress Wu Chao, A.D. 625–705 became the first ruler in China to set up a sovereign-controlled secret service. Queen Elizabeth came to power in 1558 and built espionage into an international operation that made England a major power, uniting the nation and establishing her navy, during her 45 year reign. Mata Hari is legendary. She was framed by German intelligence in WWI who used agent Walter Canaris to do so. Canaris later became Admiral Canaris who headed German intelligence in WW1I. But the story goes on when her daughter, Banda, was also shot as a spy by North Koreans thirty-three years later to the minute. She warned America that China would intervene in Korea. She was ignored. French Agent Peggy Taylor made 22 jumps behind the lines; Belgian Yvonne Files made bombs in her living room and spied; Hungarian llona at age 13 carried money behind German lines; Austrian pianist Barbara Issikides carried secret documents; Polish Countess Skarbek was caught twice but escaped both times.

Lebanon's Rima Tannous and Therese Halsa served as terrorists;

Russia's Maria, Dunaieva (the Red Mata Hari) stole American codes;

Czech teacher, Maria Gulevic saved countless OSS lives in the Czech mountains; Israel's Branda Fuch died at her post fighting the British; Germany's Baroness de Kaulla conspired in the 1800's and America's Virginia Hall went behind enemy lines with 'Cuthbert', her artificial leg, and sabotaged. Also Betty Pack who never left America but managed to get secret codes of the Italians that helped in the North Africa invasion. She kept an open bed and with safe cracking, seductive smiles and writhing hips wrote a new chapter.

Code names included Tramp, the Lark, The Cat, The Mouse. An unnamed woman worked at Peenemunde and called down a bombing raid at the time top German scientists were convened. Over 200 of them died dealing a devastating blow to Hitler. She also died, alone, unnamed and unmourned.

These stories, told by a former OSS agent who knew some of them personally, give a different look at how women have operated using their minds and all the cunningness attributed to them, not just their bodies.

Some of them died horribly at the hands of the Nazis. Toenails and teeth were pulled slowly, four were thrown alive into crematory ovens.

The special 'toys' (known as James Bond gadgetry) and black propaganda ploys (blackmail, forgery, rumor spreading), all fully described, were all at their disposal. Women have taken the unwritten book on espionage and written their own chapters. These are detailed in *Loyal and Lethal Ladies of Espionage*.

Tom Moon

A Word About Women

"Women are absolutely unfit for espionage work. They have little understanding of high politics or military affairs. Even if you use them to spy on their husbands, they do not really understand what their husbands are talking about. They are too emotional, sentimental and unreliable."

Richard Sorge, Soviet Spymaster in World War 11

Note to Mr. Sorge from the author:
May I introduce you to some special ladies.
Read on…

Tom Moon

FOREWORD

Intriguing tales of espionage and counter espionage have fascinated people for centuries. Outstanding agents in a few cases have become quite well known. The great majority of actual spies brought before the public have been men. This has caused some to disparagingly refer to the male dominance in espionage as, 'the appendage syndrome'. It has become evident espionage is one of those areas that fit women like a custom designed gown. Women, it has been proved, have their own unique way of processing and analyzing information. Their cunning and wiles have allowed them to move into areas where men have not, and most likely could not, have trod. They show an inquisitiveness and determination that does not overshadow their brothers but rather is a meaningful addition. And, where essential, they can be as ruthless as the men.Earliest recorded history shows that Empress Wu Chao, AD 625–705 was the first ruler in China to set up a sovereign-controlled secret service. Perhaps this became the basis for that of Queen Elizabeth nine centuries later. It has also been recorded that the High Priestesses at

Delphi in Greece had a simple way to pass on their intelligence. While supposedly in a drug-induced trance they passed information on amidst gibberish. And Byzantine Empress Theodora danced nude before her court while her spies worked the streets knowing the citizens minds were on other things.It was not until the sixteenth century ground work was formalized for forming secret service operations in Europe. Queen Elizabeth the First brought the art of espionage to an international level with the help and guidance of her principal secretary. Sir Francis Walshingham. In 1558 the Queen took the throne. She faced a country torn with religious dissent as well as a large debt due to her wars with France. The English people were impoverished. Forty five years later she died. During this time her country had passed through one of the greatest periods in her history. She was united as a nation and established as a first rate naval power in Europe. Her commerce and industry flourished. In addition colonization of the New World had begun.

How had she succeeded so admirably? The answer lay in a far-reaching secret service network that she and Walsingham developed jointly. She utilized her foreign ambassadors as agents. English students sent abroad reported on foreign events. Jesuit priests were subverted to spy on the political activities within their church. She was even able to utilize third world countries such as Italy for actions against her Spanish enemy. Cleverly she used her Welsh astrologer and cryptographer, John Dee, a Cambridge graduate, to influence European politicians. His astrological predictions were often subtly altered for those results the Queen wished to achieve. The same ploy of altered astrological forecasts was used by OSS against Hitler in WW11. Knowing he followed a particular astrologer he was subtly fed items to play on his paranoia. Even the ill-fated flight of Reich Deputy Rudolph Hess in 1941 was partly inspired by altered astrology predictions also.

The use of psychics continued long after Queen Elizabeth. The British secret service indicated the employment of a woman known only as Anne. She allegedly performed out-of-body trips across the channel for intelligence reasons. The OSS considered smuggling a German prisoner, in a post-hypnotic state, into Berlin to murder Hitler. U.S. Marines in Vietnam were instructed by a 'water-witch1 or dowser to locate enemy mines. The C1A at one time was interested in the use of African witch doctors. And, yes, even Nancy Reagan worked with a California seer. Hillary Clinton has been involved in talks with those who have passed beyond the veil. In particular she has sought Eleanor Roosevelt. Cross channeling and the paranormal are other areas that are being explored.

Looking at situations from the female perspective often reveals details men either overlook or consider too insignificant to pursue . One woman's determination and attentiveness to the smallest detail enabled her to pick out from aerial photos the launching sights of the Germans deadly V rockets. Bombers slowed them down.

Until the beginning of the first World War espionage was considered a dirty business. Only lowlife would stoop to it. The few women who dared to probe its depths also had the prejudice of the good old boys club to circumvent. Spying was not for women, after all.

The age-old question of a woman's intuition versus logic will never be resolved. But often intuition has unlocked secrets in a way that can be explained with only that one word.

The woman had an immediate distrust of an individual which could not be explained; the woman sensed there was danger in a pending trip or entering a room; in sizing up another woman was there something about her manner of dress or social skills that did not fit the image she was projecting.

Playing the role of the ingenue has brought more secrets from men anxious to please than a hundred cracked safes or picked pockets. Knowing how to stroke the male ego has elicited much information that would never have been obtained otherwise.

1 have known and interviewed a few of these special women. They have told their stories in a forthright and sincere way. There was no self-aggrandizement or embellishing of their roles. In all there is the common thread of dedicated, brave women giving their all for their causes. And always there is their extraordinary use of cunning and guile.

Surprisingly the use of sex does not always play the role many think it does. The ladies have found out they can do even more with their minds than their bodies.

The nations that have scoffed at the use of women as spies are the losers. The special ability to deceive that is part of a woman's character has been used with great success and deadly efficiency. Many of the ladies names were not made a part of the record and can be identified only by codenames or nicknames.

Not all of them conducted espionage. Some committed daring acts risking prison or death and are certainly worthy of inclusion. The loyalty and bravery that has caused them to put themselves at such great peril reveals their true character.Such are the women whose stories are now told.

CHAPTER I

▼

The Biblical Days

The Old Testament, certainly in male chauvinistic times, records some of the earliest tales of women's activities. When a woman could be divorced at a husbands whim and was really his property there was little they could do or say. Who would even listen to what a woman had to offer?

Delilah, who took Sampson to the cleaners (or clippers) certainly found a way. Esther saved the lives of countless of her people by risking her own life. Even Rahab, an early hooker, made history by saving the lives of two of Joshua's spies and eventually her entire family. These were hardly the 'little women1 of those times.

I
Hadassah aka Esther

She was a beautiful young Jewish girl who had been orphaned when she was quite young. She was raised by her Uncle, Mordecai. Her story from the Old Testament tells us during the third year of the reign of King Ahasuerus, emperor of the vast Media-Persia empire, he became disenchanted with his Queen, Vashti. She had refused an order to appear before him and his court.

His counsel advised him to banish her lest her refusal spill over onto other wives and they become disobedient. He did so. This set the scene for the appearance of Esther at the urging of Mordecai. The King was to select a new queen from the most beautiful young virgins available. Esther won the grand prize and became the new Queen. Mordecai advised her not to reveal she was Jewish and she did not.

Mordecai refused to bow to the Kings Prime Minister, Haman. This angered him and he convinced the King the Jews were out to subvert the Kingdom. He requested permission to kill all the Jews in the land. It was granted.

When the Jews learned of the declaration there was great wailing and sorrow. Mordecai got word to Esther that she must intercede. She advised no one could approach the King unless he held out the golden scepter and he had not called for her in over a month. She was told if she let the Jews perish she would likwise join them. Laying her life on the line she agreed. But first came the cunning that was typical of her gender.

She invited the King and Haman to a special banquet. It was to be several days away to heighten the anticipation. Haman was delighted feeling he was to be a special guest and so honored. Haman was so carried away with his plans he ordered a 75 foot high gallows from which Mordecai was to be hanged.

When the two men joined Esther she carefully laid out her plea. She pleaded for her life and those of 'her people. She said they were 'sold to those who will destroy us'. Then, knowing a large sum of money had been mentioned by Haman, she craftily added she could remain quiet if her people were only to be sold into slavery, not the death that awaited them, 'even though there would be an incalcuable damage to the king that no amount of money could begin to cover'·

The king was amazed. He demanded to know who on earth would dare to touch his Queen.

And now she played the trump card, declaring, 'This wicked Haman is our enemy'·

The King was overwrought at the perfidy of Haman and went out in the garden to calm down. Haman, knowing he was doomed, pleaded with Esther for his life. In despair he fell on the couch where Esther was reclining just as the King returned. Bad timing.

'Will he even rape the Queen right here in the palace?' he roared. Immediately the death veil was placed over his face. One of the Kings aides helpfully pointed out the 75 foot gallows Haman had constructed. He was hung on it immediately. The Jews had been saved by the beautiful Esther who laid her life on the line .

∧

II
RAHAB

We read about her in the second book of Joshua in the Old Testament. A lady of questionable repute, her name remains well known to bible readers even today.

She was not an espionage agent for she gathered no intelligence for analysis. She was simply described as a harlot who lived in a simple apartment in Jericho but played a vital role.

Joshua sent two of his men to spy out the land for he intended conquering the City. The two men were betrayed and the King of Jericho ordered them captured.

They were in Rahab1s apartment when the Kings agents came to her door saying they sought the two men who were supposedly with her. She had already hidden them in the flax on the roof and told the agents she did not know where they were.

But first she had exacted a promise from Joshua's men that for her help they would spare her and her family when they overran Jericho. They agreed.

When the great gates of Jericho shut for the night Rahab, whose apartment was on the wall, lowered the two men in a large basket and they returned to give what information they had obtained. They told him of their agreement to spare Rahab and her family. The same rope that had lowered their basket would identify the apartment and all within would be spared.

True to their agreement Rahab and all her family were the only ones not slaughtered when Jericho fell.

III
Delilah

Her name is far better known than Rahab. Her story has been told countless times over the centuries.

This early beauty from biblical times was pressed into service for her government in a unique way. They needed help in solving the problem of a super strong-man named Sampson. He had been creating havoc and terrorizing the area. No one dared stand up to him. On the physical side, the macho side, he was invincible.

The officials rationalized there had to be a better way to approach him and someone suggested the beautiful Delilah might just be the answer. With charm, cunning and sex appeal he might be tricked into revealing the secret of his great strength.

It was no problem for Delilah to get a date with him. As women do she no doubt felt his muscles and stroked his ego. She asked for tales of his daring and great victories and he was only too eager to tell of his prowess in battle.

We don't know if she checked to see if he had a work-out plan or special dietary supplements. But we do know she succeeded with female sweet talk. His defenses were totally down when he went to sleep after revealing his strength lay in his hair. That did it. The locals came in with shears and cut off his hair and just like that he lost his strength. Delilah had triumphed where the strongest man could not.

The American Revolutionary War

The use of not only espionage but covert operations was more a part of George Washington's war than realized.

Washington was his own spymaster during the war of independence. He corresponded with agents through letters written with invisible ink and created fake businesses as cover for his spies. He misled the British by planting false information. He even went so far as to plan the kidnapping of King George Ill's son.

Continuing on in that vein, Thomas Jefferson once considered burning down Saint Paul's Cathedral in London. As president he wielded clandestine agents freely against North American Indians and North African Barbary states.

Benjamin Franklin, in Paris, wrote anti-British articles. He forged a document claiming that British agents were buying bales of American scalps, including women and children, from the Indians. He also planned an attack on British commerce by privateers sailing from French ports in the hope of forcing an outraged Britain to declare war on France.

While these covert operations were being conducted at top level, the women of those days were also at work. Though held down and considered insignificant they made themselves known in countless ways. Taking advantage of their gender they could easily pass through the British lines who reasoned that they presented no danger. After all, what could a woman do or know?

Big mistake!!

They could count guns and wagons. They could piece together troop strength and often where they were headed.

Even Quaker women served in an area where they would normally be expected to be opposed. But they valued freedom enough to put aside religious beliefs temporarily.

Several major battles turned on information the ladies had been able to obtain and pass on. Messages were sewn inside cloth buttons, put in produce or buried in sacks of grain. Standing quietly and humbly our ladies of the day made their mark known in our fight for independence.

IV
Lydia Darragh

General George Washington had no official espionage network. He fed on scraps of information passed on by farmers and itinerants. Country women passing through enemy lines in search of food relied on their anonymity to return with information of value to the American cause.

While Nathan Hale, the spy caught and hanged by the British, is honored by his statue standing outside the C1A headquarters in Langley, Virginia, none exists of an equally brave hero who was not caught. She was Lydia Darragh, a Quaker.

Lydia lived with her husband, William, and family at 177 South Second Street in Philadelphia. This was across the street from the Cadwalader mansion occupied by British General William Howe and his staff. Howe had originally attempted to requisition the Darragh home. After their pleadings he agreed to use only their large parlor and then only on those special occasions when he would require more space.

In her Quaker gray habit she was never suspect. She used her 14 year old son to send messages to her oldest son, Lt. Charles Darragh who was serving with Washington at the winter headquarters at Whitemarsh, Pennsylvania.

William was likewise devoted to the American cause. He would transcribe whatever information he had been able to acquire on a scrap of paper. Lydia would then sew them inside the large cloth buttons common in those days. Attaching the buttons to her sons clothes he would then slip through British lines to deliver them.

But her curiosity paid off on December 1, 1777 when General Howe ordered them to evacuate their parlor for his use. She remained behind to eavesdrop and picked up some valuable information regarding a surprise attack on Washington's forces planned by the British two nights later.

Time did not permit the customary method of transmitting such information. Husband William could not get out of Philadelphia with the British now on full alert.

It was Lydia who said she alone could do it.

Early the next morning an inconspicuous Quaker lady threw a grain bag over her shoulder and started through British lines ostensibly to visit the grain mills. It was a long, cold walk.

She found Colonel Elias Boudinot, one of Washington's aides in the Rising Sun Tavern in Whitemarsh. He later reported, "A poor, insignificant little woman walked up to me and put in my hands a dirty old needlework with various small pockets sewed inside". Those pockets revealed that Howe was going to attack Washington's headquarters on December 4th with 5,999 men, 13 pieces of cannon, baggage, weapons and 11 boats on wagon wheels. Alerted to this pending attack Washington was ready. The British were defeated.

Others Who Served
V
Peggy Shippen

Λ

Some other American women cast their lot with the British. One was the young wife of Major Benedict Arnold. As Peggy Shippen, daughter of a prominent Tory family. she had been the toast of Philadelphia. After marrying Arnold she convinced him to betray the American cause» She acted as his secretary in his plot to seize West Point. Eventually she followed him into exile in England·

VI
Patience Mehitabel Lovell Wright

As war broke out with England Patience Mehitabel Lovell Wright began her service in London as an intelligence agent. She was a sculptress and confidant of Benjamin Franklin. She had achieved fame for creating life-like portrayals of prominent people. In that her studios became a fashionable meeting place for the nobility as well as the King and Queen she was able to obtain many facts and secrets. She was forced to flee London in early 1776.

Other references to unnamed women who risked their lives and fortune to aid the American cause are found but unfortunately neither Washington or his lieutenants listed their names. Whether from chivalry or chauvinism will never be known.

The Franco Prussian War
VII
Baroness Madame De Kaulla

The genesis of Germany's espionage service began in the 1860's under the tutelage of William Stieber. As Chief of Prussian Intelligence he was so well known his services were embraced in Japan where he was regarded him as the ultimate in intelligence gathering. He founded the Green House which was established to provide every possible type of sexual operation including deviancy. Its primary purpose was to recruit those people for service who under ordinary circumstances had no desire to do so

Like a chess master he matched his beautiful women with various foreign officials. One such woman was Baroness Madame de Kaulla who had been a delightful diversion for French General de Cissey when he was captured by the Germans during the Franco-Prussian war in 1870.

The RHIP (rank has its privileges) factor was solidly in place then as now and the General was 'incarcerated' in a beautiful villa near Hamburg. For companionship he was introduced to the Baroness who helped him while away his lonely hours—and nights. With the war ending the General returned to his native France. Many years later Stieber learned France was reorganizing its forces. General Cissey was now Minister of War. Why not send the Baroness to renew old acquaintances, he surmised.

It became a nightly affair as the General rushed to her apartment for her company and discussed the affairs of the day. Watching the goings on was French Intelligence, well aware of what was happening—but again invoking the RH1P factor. They could only hope the General was being circumspect. Not wanting to embarrass their Minister of War, the Baroness was not prosecuted.

The Civil War

The war between the states came much as two little boys pushing, shoving and threatening one another. Neither expected a fight would actually occur. Neither side was prepared for it as the north with the industry and greater population looked on the upstart southern states almost with amusement.

The south had no army. The army of the United States numbered about 16,000 and was spread out over the west with its Indian problems.

This war was filled with exploits of women who bore almost indescribable hardships espousing their cause. Many posed as men and fought in small skirmishes and major battles. Many were killed on the battlefield.So many women posed as men the officers had to do simple tests for female mannerisms. An apple thrown to a woman posing as a man would often give her away as she reached for her imaginary apron to catch it. The way in which women put on their stockings also gave many of them away. Yet another woman was discovered at Camp Cook, Cleveland when she gave an unmistakable twist to the dishcloth in wringing it out that no masculine could ever counterfeit.

Because of the southern lack of manpower, industry and munitions it was essential to learn as much of the enemy as possible and that meant using spies.

Neither side knew much about espionage and certainly nothing about counter-espionage. Citizens on both sides moved freely getting information and passing it back to their respective governments. The common citizen did much of the work in obtaining bits and pieces of information in his/her spare time. But there were some who devoted their careers to spying and went about the business with varying degrees of success.

More myths exist about spies during this period than any other. Since records were poorly kept and many destroyed, it is difficult to properly assess who did what and the importance of their activities.

Edwin C. Fishel wrote an article entitled, "The Mythology of Civil War Intelligence" pointing out most of the tales of Civil War spies had less than a nodding acquaintance with the truth. He felt that usually they were imaginative products of the "moonlight and magnolia" school of history.

What is known is that there were two rival intelligence organizations in the north. One was headed by Alien Pinkerton and reported to General McClellan, commander of the Army of the Potomac. The other was under the command of General Winfield Scott and reported to the Secretary of State. All too frequently the members of one group arrested someone from the other and problems had to be ironed out.

In the south there were similar problems but president Jefferson Davis, personally ran intelligence and counter-espionage operations.

Codes and ciphers the agents had to be used were rudimentary and easily broken.

The situation was made for female agents. The age of chivalry still existed. No one would suspect a woman of doing such a dastardly thing as spying. A bit of male chauvinism must have also been part of the picture for it was thought a woman would certainly not be capable of doing such a thing anyway.

Enter now those women we know something of who served on both sides of our Civil War.

CHAPTER 2

▼

VIII
Elizabeth Van Lew Aka "Crazy Bet"

In 1864 one of the most important Union agents was a frail bird-like spinster, Elizabeth Van Lew. Referred to as 'Miss Lizzie', she was labeled as slightly mad. Living in and operating from Richmond she was said at one point to be, "…all that was left of the power of the United States Government in Richmond…the greater part of our intelligence we owed to the intelligence and devotion of Miss Van Lew". This according to Colonel George Sharpe, head of the Bureau of Military Information•

Carrying out her dangerous missions nearly resulted in her arrest on more than one occasion.

As a member of a well known Virginia family she lived with her parents in a beautiful mansion. It was across the street from the historic church where Patrick Henry had made his famous declaration about, 'liberty or death'.

She referred to Virginians as 'our people' and certainly should have been a staunch secessionist. Instead she was dedicated to abolishing slavery and lived it in her every action. Many said it was no doubt due to her northern roots when her father moved his family to Richmond from Long Island. He then opened a prosperous hardware store. Her mother was from Philadelphia.

Elizabeth was born in 1818 and was described as a pretty child with 'lively blue eyes'. Her dedication to the abolition of slavery surfaced early. At her fathers death she immediately freed all nine family slaves. She declared, "Slave power is arrogant, is jealous and intrusive is cruel, is despotic, not only for the slave, but over the community, the state".

In addition she added, "Slave power degrades labor".

When she learned slaves owned by others who were related to the former Van Lew slaves were being sold, she bought and freed them also.

While her views were certainly known to her friends they all thought she would get over it.

When the Civil War broke out she was living alone with her widowed mother in their large house. She seemed isolated but her abolitionist views never altered

At the age of 46 she suddenly came to life as the Civil War broke in all its fury. On a bluff below here home the Confederates established Libby Prison in an old warehouse. Lizzie and her mother defied, confounded and angered their neighbors by regular visits to the Union soldiers imprisoned there. They supplied them with food, clothing, medicine and comfort. In many instances Elizabeth persuaded Confederate doctors the sicker soldiers should be transferred to hospitals which was done.

A local newspaper article declared, "Whilst every true woman in this community was busy making articles for our troops, or administering to our sick, these two women have been spending their opulent means in aiding and giving comfort to the miscreants who have invaded our sacred soil, bent on rapine and murder." Had they known the true story there might have been a lynching or at least a prison cell for the women.

The prisoners began slipping her information, most of which she did not understand. But she was in contact with Union agents who came into the city regularly and well understood the value of her information•

The procedure became more sophisticated when questions between Union agents and the prisoners were passed back and forth hidden in food baskets or even wrapped up with medicine bottles. With the need to converse with new prisoners for up to date intelligence she often had others engage the guards with talk while she probed the new men for more information. When she was forbidden to talk with them any longer she arranged to bring them books. They would use tiny pin pricks in the latter pages to transfer their information.

She employed a double-bottom dish designed to hold hot water which contained notes instead. One day a guard who had been observing her comings and goings demanded to see the dish. She obligingly handed it from under her shawl. The guard howled and dropped it for this time it contained boiling water.

Because she was being questioned more and more, even followed, she adopted a new ploy. Playing on her reputation as being a bit eccentric she stopped taking care of herself. She no longer combed or brushed her hair. She wore tattered clothing and mismatched shoes. People soon called her "Crazy Bet". But it paid off when she was left more and more alone to ply her craft.

Her only rebuke came when suddenly her permit to visit the prison was revoked. At this point she called on an old family friend, then the Provost Marshal of Richmond. He scolded her mildly for her conduct but did sign a new permit. Her work went on and became more and more important as the war increased. The Union gave her her own cipher. She hid the key to it in her watch case. Union agents used her home as a safe haven. When given special incriminating papers she hid them in the andirons in her bedroom.

The surveillance began to increase and she saw strange faces around her property. Sometimes she was aware of being followed. Tiring of surprise searches she had a most ingenious plan. When it was announced there was to be a new Commander of Libby Prison she invited him and his wife to move in to her home. He gladly agreed and never was aware what was going on around him. Earlier work paid off in the form of a former Van Lew slave, bought and freed by Elizabeth who recognized her intelligence and sent her north to be educated.

When the war broke out she sent for the girl, Mary Elizabeth Bowser, and asked her to return to Richmond. She then inducted her into the spy ring and got her a job in Jefferson Davis's home. There Mary eavesdropped on his conversation and went through his personal papers supplying valuable information. Communications reached new venues as messages were carried via the five way stations between the Van Lew home and the north.

Sometimes they were put in hollowed eggs, sometimes stitched in the pattern of a dress. Another subterfuge was an innocent letter written to an 'uncle' which contained messages in invisible ink.

When the war reached Richmond and the city was greatly damaged by the fires set by retreating soldiers. Lizzie was ready. She broke out her huge flag with 34 stars and unfurled it in front of her home—the first American flag to fly there in over four years.

Angry neighbors gathered threatening to tear down the flag and burn her home. Defiant to the end she came out and confronted them. She called many of them by name, shook her finger and said if anything did happen to her the Union troops would avenge her. They withdrew.

Her work was not forgotten by General Grant. Even before Richmond fell he sent in an advance guard to protect her. When they arrived they found her poking around in the burned out ruins of the Confederate capitol searching for special documents that had not burned in the fire.

Almost immediately upon his arrival Grant called on the lady. Gone was "Crazy Bet" and in her place Miss Elizabeth Van Lew, a respectably attired lady with combed hair greeted him. They had tea on her veranda.

To express his gratitude Grant made her postmistress of Richmond. He further endorsed a proposal to award her $15,000 for her services. Congress failed to approve it. She became dependent on funds from friends of the prisoners whose lives she had saved.

She never left Richmond and died there in 1900 at the age of 82.

∧

IX
Sarah Emma Edmonds
aka Frank Thompson

No doubt one of the strangest (and most dangerous) missions taken on by a Federal agent was that of
Sarah Edmonds. Her father had wanted boys. She was
the fifth and last child of her parents. Wanting to satisfy her father she wore boys clothes and took on the
hardest chores on their farm. She could outride and
outshoot most boys her age. She was stubborn, determined and reckless.

She hailed from New Brunswick and entered the U.S.
in 1856. Drawn to the pioneer spirit she spent some time
in the west but went to Washington, D.C. when the Civil
War broke out. She served as a nurse and at the battle of
Bull Run treated wounded and dying soldiers.

When the attack on Fort Monroe was begun under
McClellan she joined his forces. As the battle began
shaping up the soldiers on both sides dug new
trenches across the old ones from the Revolutionary
battle at Yorktown.

Going the extra mile in her service to the Union, she
went into the field to forage for food. The shifting battle lines often caused soldiers to go hungry. On one of
these trips she came across a Confederate woman who
fired a pistol at her in an attempt to kill her. The
woman had lost her husband, father and two brothers
in the fighting.

Emma had left a young man in New Brunswick she
was in love with. He too had come south and joined in
the fighting. After one of her many foraging expeditions

she learned he had been killed. She returned to her camp just in time to see the return of his burial party.

Now it was payback time for what had so far been an army nurse. Wanting to strike back she volunteered to become a spy. In military records she was listed as Frank Thompson. She was closely examined as to her intentions and, when they were satisfied, given three days to figure her disguise. Her plan was unheard of. Not only would she change her gender, she would change her race. She would enter Confederate lines as a black man.

She began by having her head shaved. To color her skin she used nitrate of silver covering every inch of her visible skin. She purchased a plantation style outfit to complete our outfit. But she still lacked the right hair. Deciding she must have a wig of real negro wool she went to a ship about to leave and approached a postmaster she knew. He did not recognize her and asked what he might do for this "poor old darkie". To try out her dialect she said, "Massa send me to you wid dis yere money for you to fotch him a darkie wig from Washington". Though puzzled he did as requested and shortly she was ready for her trip into Confederate territory.

Setting out after dark she quickly walked through the picket lines of both armies. She had no blanket or provisions other than a few biscuits and a loaded revolver. After passing far enough behind the picket lines to feel safe she lay down to pass the night in the forest. The next morning she encountered a Negro work party. They were taking provisions to the picket line.

When she identified herself as one of them they gave her some hot coffee to take off the nights chill and some cornbread. They went on to their appointed rounds and she stood alone but not for long.

A Confederate officer approached and asked who she belonged to and why she was not working.

In her dialect she said, "I dusn't belong to nobody, Massa. I'se free and allers was. I'se gwyne to Richmond".

He replied there were no free "niggers" and took her to a work party where she was ordered to work on a fortification. She was handed a pickaxe and wheelbarrow. Not having the muscular build of the men she experienced considerable difficulty handling her wheelbarrow. Others joined to help her.

The rations for the blacks were considerably less than the whites. She endured this more easily than the physical exertion of trying to keep up with the men.

Her quick mind catalogued and retained the armament at the Fort: fifteen three inch rifled cannon, eighteen four-and-a-half inch rifled cannon, twenty nine thirty-two pounders, twenty one forty-two pounders, thirty six Columbiads, nine Dahlgrens and seven siege howitzers. She combined this information on a rough sketch of the Fort, then secreted it in her shoe.

The next morning as she worked alongside the other slaves. One of them observed her closely, then said, "I'll be darned if that feller ain't turnin' white; if he ain't, I'm no nigger".

To defuse the situation as others looked on she said she had a white mother.

As soon as she was alone she took the last of her nitrate of silver to make sure the lightened skin was black once more.

At one point, while filling the canteens of some soldiers, she heard a familiar voice. It was a peddler who came to the Union camp weekly with various items for sale. He would spend a lot of time talking with the Union soldiers.

She overheard him giving a full report on the size and layout of the Union camp. Then brag about the death of a Union scout he had betrayed to Confederate snipers.

She made up her mind he would pay with his life—and later saw that he did.

It was obvious the Confederates were losing men when she was ordered to become a picket and handed a rifle. Her orders were to shoot anyone coming from the enemy's lines. Waiting till dark she quickly slipped across the lines and headed for friendly territory. Hoisting her pre-agreed signal she entered safely.

After surrendering her weapon to a general she knew, but who did not recognize her, she returned to her tent. She then chalked her face and put on the outfit she had worn on her examination day. In reporting she received the hearty congratulations of McClellan who gladly received her report.

Her second infiltration was that of an Irish peddler woman named Bridget. She swam the Chickahominy river and spent three chilled days in a malaria infested swamp trying to find her way out. She stumbled on a house and inside found a dying rebel soldier. He had developed typhoid fever and could not keep up with his squad. He had dragged himself into the house and, too weak to fend for himself, awaited death. He told her where to find cornmeal and flour. She made some hoe cakes and tea and satisfied his hunger before her own.

He seemed to improve, then weakened and just before his death asked her to take his gold watch to Major McKee of General Ewell's staff. He died that night, cradled in her arms.

Before leaving the house she perfected her disguise with articles from the house. She used mustard, pepper, an old pair of green glasses and a bottle of red ink. She made a plaster and put it on her face until it blistered, painted a red line around her face, rubbed dark yellow clay over her face and pulled up her hood. Filling her basket with odds and ends from the house she proceeded south to the headquarters of Major McKee. As she reached the picket line she took out her handkerchief filled with black pepper and dabbed her eyes. The sad looking woman with a tear streaked face was waved through by the picket. She found the Major, gave him the watch and a report on the now dead soldier.

She infiltrated the Confederate lines eleven times using the guise of a female contraband, a dry goods clerk and a young confederate boy. At one point she came upon a badly wounded soldier. She was taken by his beautiful eyes and as she talked to him she realized it was a woman. Her only brother had been killed and the woman didn't want it known to others she was a woman. She prayed with the dying woman and, at her request, laid her to rest on the hill where she had fallen. She later wrote a book about her experiences entitled, "Unsexed, or the Female Soldier". Later, feeling the title a bit raw for the times, it was retitled, 'Nurse and Spy."

X
Rose Greenhow

Rose O'Neal Greenhow moved graciously and effortlessly through the maze of Washington, D.C. during the Civil War. She was the widow of Dr. Robert Greenhow who died in 1854. Through him she had traveled extensively and had a liberal education in medicine, art, diplomacy and history.

Her fine home in Washington offered comfort and pleasure to many but was under suspicion due to her outspoken Confederate sympathies. Far more than that, she was a Confederate secret agent. In the capital she was often known as Rebel Rose.

Her greatest coup led to a Union debacle. Her courier service penetrated all aspects of Union security. She advised Confederate General Beauregard that General Irvin McDowell was marching on Manassas, Virginia. The manner in which her message was delivered could not have been better scripted by Hollywood.

A pretty young acquaintance of Rebel Rose, Betty Duvall, crossed into the front lines southwest of Washington. She was appropriately attired as a country girl in calico and bounced up and down on a produce wagon. The wagon pulled into a friends home where Duvall changed into a trim riding habit and left the next morning. She was headed toward the Confederate advance post at the Fairfax Court House.

When she reached General M. L. Bonham she reached back and removed a comb from her long hair. It tumbled down around her hips as she removed a small pocket watch sized package that was sewn up in silk. It contained a brief message from Rose Greenhow advising General McDowell would advance in mid-July. The date she gave the message to the General was July 10, 1861.

With this information the Confederates adjusted their lines and handed the Union a severe defeat. Her timely ciphered message set the stage for the Union defeat at Bull Run in 1861.

Other reports were not as kind suggesting her message was of importance but not the sole reason for the Union defeat.

Seven years after her husbands death she assessed her attributes. Her beauty was beginning to fade but she still had that incredible charm that enabled her to work men like soft putty according to one story.

What Greenhow did not know was that the Secretary of War, Thomas Scott, had asked a newly appointed security man, Alan Pinkerton, to watch her house closely. His instructions were to observe all who came and went and that anyone leaving should come under close surveillance. Pinkerton was to report to Scott daily until told otherwise. The noose was being fashioned and would soon be tightened.

Her home was at the corner of Thirteenth and I streets. It was two stories in height with a large front staircase.

Pinkerton relates a delightful tale of standing on his men's shoulders during a driving rainstorm to peer in the windows. What he did see was an army officer conferring with Mrs. Greenhow and going over some papers he assumed were military secrets.

When the officer left Pinkerton tailed him. He identified him as a Union officer and so reported to Scott. The officer was indeed giving information to the lady and was subsequently court-martialed. Pinkerton continued his surveillance.

Eight days later Mrs. Greenhow was placed under house arrest. All of her papers were taken by the government. She continued, however, trying to get messages to the Confederacy and finally was placed in the Old Capitol Prison for several months. For unknown reasons she was released and traveled south to the rebel capital.. Here she was acclaimed.

On August 5, 1863, she left North Carolina on a blockade runner. In her trunk was a manuscript of her espionage activities entitled "My Imprisonment and the First Year of Abolition Rule at Washington". It became an immediate success for the cause of the Confederacy as well as considerable funds. In Europe she continued bitter attacks on the north.

At the end of August 1864 she returned to America aboard the blockade runner Condor. The ship ran aground outside the Confederate Fort Fisher as it tried to go around a ship that had grounded there several days earlier.

The weather was miserable with heavy mists and rain. Through it Mrs. Greenhow saw an approaching Union ship. In spite of the heavy seas, remembering the unpleasantness of her prior incarceration, she demanded she put over the side in a boat.

The Captain complied and observed a huge breaker striking the boat broadside and capsizing it.

The London Daily Mail printed an article from a Confederate sympathizer telling how the men in the overturned boat all managed to save themselves by hanging onto the keel of the boat. In the uproar of the surf and wind nothing was seen or heard of Mrs. Greenhow until her body was found the next day. For some reason a pouch containing $2,500 in gold was around her neck which, no doubt, caused her to sink immediately.

A final detail was added by a Confederate soldier who found the money on the beach and kept it. When he learned it had come from the celebrated Mrs. Greenhow he turned it in.

XI
Belle Boyd

There were opposing views of another well known woman who served during the Civil War.

She was Belle Boyd and her spy career began with a bang when she was only 17. She lived in Martinsburg in the northern part of the Shenandoah Valley near Harpers Ferry.

The war had just begun. On July 4, 1861 some Union soldiers got drunk and decided it would be a good thing to remove the rebel flag from her home. One said something extremely crude to her mother whereupon Belle shot him dead.

She was acquitted.

She went to work with a vengeance noting troop movements and strength and reporting them to the Confederates. As a rank amateur she failed to use a code or even disguise her handwriting. When caught she was again acquitted. Chivalry was her greatest asset .

On May 23, 1862, Belle was with some relatives in her home when a servant rushed in to report the Confederate forces were arriving. She went out to talk with a retreating Federal officer who advised they were about to burn their warehouses and bridges, retreat north and link up with General Banks' troops. She went to a balcony and with glasses observed forward elements of the Confederate forces approaching. She was unusually concerned over the fate of the Confederates, not only because they were marching into an ambush, but because she knew her father was with them. She had information that the southern commanders desperately needed but didn't now how to get it to them.

Going outside she found some men who had expressed sympathy for the south. She asked one of them to take a message to General Jackson. Their reply was, "Then you go".

Wearing a simple housedress she threw on a sun bonnet, grabbed a horse and took off through the fields. The Federals saw her riding and fired on her. As she approached Confederate lines they likewise shot at her but fate was with her. She arrived unharmed in the Confederate main body and there saw an old family friend. Major Harry Douglas.

Astounded at seeing her in the thick of battle he listened as she gave him disposition of Federal forces. He rushed off to alert Jackson and change strategy.

The Confederates won a substantial victory. She returned to her home.

On July 29, 1862 she was arrested by the U.S. Secret Service and taken to the infamous Libby Prison. Here she was treated with the utmost respect. On August 28th she was dismissed from the prison. No specific charges could be proved.

Upon her return to Richmond she was cheered and hailed as a true heroine. In May 1864 she traveled to England and wrote her memoirs. She married a Union naval officer and converted him to the southern cause.

She described herself as "a beautiful cloaked courier racing on horseback up and down the Shenandoah Valley by night for the Confederate cause".

Others reported she was simply a rawboned country girl who was lucky and conveyed only one message of importance to the south. A photograph of her revealed a woman with protruding teeth and a sharp nose. One soldier unkindly said she could eat a tomato through a picket fence.

Her most treasured momento was a letter of gratitude from General Stonewall Jackson thanking her for her services.

After the war she went on the stage playing straight roles in the popular dramas of the day. She died in 1900 in Kilbourn, Wisconsin.

XII
Harriet Tubman Aka 'Moses'

It was 1849 when Harriet Tubman escaped from slavery. A black woman, she was born and raised in slavery and had little future during this period of American history.

She was given the name of Araminta at birth but changed it to Harriet, her mother's name. Grandparents from both sides had arrived in America in chains.

In 1844 she married a free black man, John Tubman. Whether he was with her or not when she escaped to Philadelphia five years later is not clear. What is clear was her never wavering intent to free other slaves regardless of the cost.

Prior to the Civil War she formed and led one of the most successful underground railroads leading hundreds of escaped slaves to safe havens in the north. She was so effective a price was offered for her capture.

Frederick Douglass, a noted black anti-slavery spokesman said, "I know of no one who has willingly encountered more perils and hardships to serve our enslaved people than you have". She became known as 'Moses' to those she had led to freedom.

A religious woman she nevertheless carried a pistol. It was both for defense but also a prodder for those slaves who became too discouraged facing the hardships ahead for them. She would tell them, "Dead niggers tell no tales, you go on or die".

A gifted strategist she faced many hardships but used her skills to eventually get 300 slaves new homes. During these years she became the first black woman to speak out for women's rights. It was said John Brown consulted with her prior to his famous raid on Harper's Ferry.

Then came the war. She went to work for the Union in the south serving as a nurse, scout and finally spy. She led a corps of black troops on several missions into Confederate territory. She was an excellent communicator with her black brothers.

Her most famous raid came in June 1863 when she went up the Combahee River on several missions and at the same time managed to free over 700 blacks leading them north to freedom.

Though uneducated she could evaluate information from the slaves to pass on to Union forces. In addition she could analyze the military strategy of forces opposing her making her even more valuable as a spy.

As the war ended she returned to her home in Auburn, New York and spent her final years there.

But this active, dynamic woman did not retire to a rocking chair. She continued being an activist for women's rights and seeking dignity and respect for black women and all former slaves. It was said of her, "•...Harriet Tubman was an extraordinary human being, and probably the most underrated and underappreciated person of either sex or any race from the Civil War period."

XIII
Loreta Janeta Velazquez
Aka LT. Harry T. Buford

Sitting tall in the saddle, head back and riding with fellow officers Lt• Harry T. Buford looked northward to Union forces preparatory to the battle of Bull Run.

It was July 20, 1861 and Lt. Buford prepared for the thrill of his first battle. Except it was really her first battle for underneath the fake beard and mustache was actually a Cuban born woman, Loreta Janeta Velazquez.

She was raised in New Orleans in a well to do family. Her childhood dreams had been of doing great things. Her heroine was Joan of Arc. The first battles showed her the horror of war. "To be a second Joan of Arc was a mere girlish fancy which my very first experiences as a soldier dissipated forever...," she confessed.

A black servant named Bob, unaware Buford was actually a woman, traveled with her. The unnecessary slaughter brought out her feminine side and she felt there must be a better way to serve the south.

Borrowing clothes from a negro woman she became a woman once more. Perhaps spying would be more suited to her.

She went to Washington, D.C. and mingled with both civilians and soldiers there. It was all too easy obtaining information from soldiers anxious to talk to a woman. This convinced her she would make an excellent spy.

She returned to the negro lady, returned her clothes and picked up her uniform once more. Now as Lt. Buford she was ready for a new job.

She rejoined Bob and together they set out for Columbus, Tennessee to seek a new job from General Leonidas Polk. She was assigned to the detective corps on a rail line checking papers and orders of those traveling.

This lasted but a few weeks. She was drawn back into battle and, together with Bob, fought at Fort Donelson. She was wounded in the foot. Now tired and in pain she withdrew for some badly needed rest. She and Bob went to New Orleans.

That city was tense with the Fort Donelson defeat and looking for spies. Her guard had dropped over the long time in service and she was shocked when she was arrested and charge with being a woman. She denied it, went to trial and was found to be a woman. After spending ten days in jail (other records indicate three months) she was released.

She got out of New Orleans as soon as possible to avoid the increasing publicity her case had engendered.

The quickest way was to reenlist in the army, this time as a private. She was gladly received in the 21st Louisiana Regiment.

One of those quirks of fate arose when she reported to a Captain Thomas C. DeCaulp who knew Lt. Buford from earlier days. He was delighted to see his old friend. The fascinating fact was DeCaulp had known Loreta as the wife of a friend who was later killed. He had courted Loreta by mail and the two considered themselves to be engaged. He did not know that Lt. Buford and Loreta were the same person.

In various skirmishes she became severely wounded by a mortar shell. It made her right arm useless and she was sent back for treatment•

The doctor who examined her seemed quite perplexed as he studied a severely wounded arm and shoulder of what had to be a woman. Finally she told him her story and swore him to secrecy.

Once treated she pressed on to Grenada, then Jackson where she became too ill to go on. She returned to New Orleans just as that city fell to the Union. Discarding her uniform she became a woman once more. She realized she could be of more service as a spy.

Ingratiating herself with the occupying Federal officers she won their confidence by expressing pro-Union sentiments. In short order she was given permission to pass through Union lines.

Becoming a blockade runner she traveled to Cuba where she returned with badly needed drugs and supplies. Her cover story was that of an English woman, sympathetic to the south, whose papers she had borrowed. As a British subject she had greater freedom.

A Confederate officer was caught carrying messages given to him by Loreta. He confessed and implicated her. Calling on her fake papers she called on the British consul for help who promptly got their British subject released.

She headed for Richmond but the word was out to look for any stranger and especially a woman posing as a man. A detective had her arrested and she was incarcerated in Castle Thunder prison. Her luck held as the warden and his wife befriended her, learned her story and interceded for her with General Winder. She agreed to join the secret service of the Union and was sent on a trial test which she passed.

Her wound was bothering her greatly and made her easier to spot. She was again arrested for being a woman in Lynchburg. In her prison cell she continued denying all charges. She had worked for so long in picking up male mannerisms she felt confident for all save a physical exam.

Sitting in her cell she heard footsteps and realized some new inquisitors were on the way. Adapting to male customs she put her feet up on the sill, then turned and spit on the floor just as a woman and her daughter bent on questioning her entered. That was enough to disgust them and they left without further questions, convinced only a man would do that.

Unable to prove their case the Union released her. She immediately returned to the south and in a series of events portrayed herself as a sister seeking her brother, then a wife seeking her husband in various Union prisons. She picked up information from loose talking soldiers and relayed it to her own side.

Word reached her that her 'fiance', Captain DeCaulp, was recuperating in an Atlanta hospital. Determined to once and for all reveal her true identity she went to see him. But first she wanted to hear from his own lips a true expression of his love.

DeCaulp was delighted to see Buford and they reminisced about past battles. Then DeCaulp took out a photograph of Velazquez and expressed his love. He said he had not seen her for three long years.

Though burning with a desire to end it all she played it out a little longer. She took the photograph he had, held it up to him and asked if he was sure he hadn't seen anyone like that recently.

He looked again, then shook his head sadly.

"Well, Captain, don't you think the picture of your lady-love looks the least bit like your friend, Lt. Buford"?

It struck home. He gasped and leaned back, perspiration breaking out on his forehead.

"Can it possibly be that you are she"?

Nodding she spoke of her fears that he might not appreciate the fact she had masqueraded all these years as a man.

"1 love you ten times more than ever for this, Loreta".

They were married a short time later. He felt better and reported to his command. Before he reached his post he had a relapse, then was captured. He died in a Federal hospital.

Devastated by his death she threw herself even more into the war. In New York City she registered at the Taylor Hotel as Mrs. Sue Battle. She felt the circle closing in on her as Colonel Baker who headed Federal Intelligence had assigned men to run her down.

On a train carrying incriminating documents and a large sum of money she froze as a man who she felt was following her sat down beside her. He talked briefly with a conductor and she overheard him say, "I'll catch her yet".

Realizing he did not know what she looked like she decided to find out just how much was known about her. To her dismay he painted an accurate picture.

When they left the train the detective gallantly carried her large bag with the money and documents, handed them to her and wished her luck.

Returning from her courier mission she went directly into the headquarters of Colonel Baker for some instructions. It was there he told her of a female spy traveling between Richmond and Canada they were unable to locate. He said that perhaps he would assign her to run down this elusive woman. She smiled inwardly at the thought of being hired to catch herself.

She continued switching her gender role back and forth and engaged in some major schemes to break Confederate soldiers out of prisons but the war ended before any of them came to fruition.

After the war she explored the possibility of setting up a Confederate colony in Venezuela but found too many fortune seekers and swindlers and gave it up.

In 1876 she wrote her memoirs which were published as "The Woman In Battle".

She disappeared from the records somewhere in Texas in about 1880. Because of the incredible tales many have suspected outright falsification or at least considerable embellishment of her stories•

In 'Who Was Who in the Confederacy' Stewart Safakis states after painstaking research much of her story can be confirmed. Many names, dates and places fit in with her story. Others such as conflicting dates or places could be explained as loss of memory. Many other details cannot be verified one way or the other. But overall he feels the basic stories do fit historical records. What can be said of Loreta Janeta Valezquez and all others who fought in the Civil War, both as soldiers and spies, was that the Civil War was a liberating force for bold or adventurous women seeking new horizons in the 1860s.

Others Who Served
XIV
Nancy Hart

She was another West Virginian fighting for the south. She provided Jackson's cavalry with useful information and led patrols through Union positions in the mountains. Once when she was captured she wrested her guard's musket from him, smashed him over the head with the stock and shot him dead. She escaped to serve the Confederacy as a scout.

XV
Rebecca Wright

But the Union was not without its own lethal ladies. Rebecca Wright was a Quaker school teacher in Winchester, Virginia. She received a letter from General P. H. Sheridan asking if she might inform him of the position of Early's forces, the number of divisions and his probable or reported intentions. He asked if any more troops had arrived from Richmond.

The contact was made with the help of an elderly black man who had a confederate pass to sell his vegetables to inhabitants of her town. The messages were written on tissue paper, wrapped in tin foil and secreted in the man's mouth. Miss Wright informed him the rebel troops had been returned to Richmond and that the force remaining was much smaller than reported.

This prompted him to attack and defeat the confederate forces there. After the battle he was conducted to her home to personally thank her. At wars end he sent her a beautiful gold watch with an inscription commemorating her services in 1864.

XVI
Pauline Cushman

A striking Creole actress, Pauline Cushman of New Orleans performed with itinerant Nashville state companies. The Union recruited her to obtain information on rebel territory 50 miles southeast of Nashville. She was successful in penetrating the area and obtained information on a planned attack by General Baxton Bragg. Shortly after transmitting her intelligence she was captured. Later, freed from prison, she continued her work for the Union. Her knowledge of the back roads of the southern states was of great value to the Yankee troops.

XVII
Sarah Thompson

A war widow, Sarah Thompson was responsible for
the elimination of one of Dixie's most colorful rene-
gades. Major John Hunt Morgan. The war was ending.
Atlanta had fallen. Major Morgan, however, was still
leading his hard riding company known as Morgan's
Raiders. He had taken over Greensville, Tennessee and
gone into the town to visit a friend. He was spotted by 25
year old Thompson. That night she talked her way
through southern lines, rode into a fierce thunderstorm
to Bull's Gap where she reported to Union forces. A cavalry unit was dispatched to Greenville where Morgan
was apprehended and killed.

XVIII
Dr. Mary Edwards Walker

The first woman to serve in the Union forces was Dr.
Mary Edwards Walker. She was also the first woman to
win the Medal of Honor. She was the only woman prisoner of war exchanged for a man of equal rank. At
Chattanooga, Tennessee, she served as a scout. Often she
infiltrated enemy territory to gather vital information
for General Sherman. He recommended her for the
Medal of Honor.

World War I

Through the centuries England proved its ability to
get 'down and Dirty'. Masters of duplicity, the double
cross and effective use of propaganda (especially including spreading of rumors) they showed the world how
effective it could be.

Women were now being more accepted as spies—except in America. England appeared to be heading the field in the use of women for such purposes •

Admiral Sir Reginald 'Blinker' Hall was Director of British Naval Intelligence. He had simple rules for women agents: his women must be daughters or sisters of naval officers, they must know at least two languages and they had to be able to type. The exact scope of their intelligence duties was not defined.

Unfortunately no records of these women or their activities were kept which was quite the opposite of the WWII women. There are some stories that survived but it is obvious the ladies were becoming more and more clever and sophisticated in gathering intelligence and not all of it was done in bed.

The one most famous of all female spies, Mata Hari, appears to not have been a spy at all and the manner in which she was set up by Germany was clever enough to bring about her death by a firing squad .

CHAPTER 3

▼

XIX
Jeanne Henrriette DE
Bettignies a.k.a Alice Dubois

A most versatile and clever woman served under the British Bureau during World War 1. She was Louise Marie Jeanne Henriette de Bettignies, the daughter of a porcelain manufacturer. She had a penchant for organization. The spy network she established from Artois, north to Dunkirk and into Brussels eventually posed a very real threat to the German forces in that area.

She was educated at Oxford and spoke French, Flemish, Italian, German and English. Before the war she was a governess to children of nobility in Italy and Austria. She was in Lille when the Germans marched in. She escaped to England in 1915 with valuable information about the Germans. She then volunteered her services to the British and was accepted. Lacking a training school she drew information from experienced intelligence officers in codes, secret inks, safe drops and the formation of an underground. She was given the code name of Alice Dubois. Her network was called the Alice Service.

Returning to her home in Lille Alice Dubois worked under many disguises. She was a lace seller, a peasant girl selling cheese, a school teacher. She sent messages inside Rosaries, in the headgear of the Sisters of Charity, inside candy bar wrappers, in glass eyes and wooden legs. The Alice Service smuggled allied prisoners across borders, gathered information on German troop movements, identified German installations and order of battle. The Germans arrested her in 1916 with a purse bulging with faked ID cards. She was imprisoned at St. Giles prison in Brussels where she died. Without her organizational ability the entire network slowly disintegrated.

Today in a Lille garden there is a statue to this woman erected after the first world war. Sadly those standing before it can in no way appreciate the courage, dedication and brilliance of this woman•

XX
Marthe McKenna

She lived through two major wars. Having been born as Martha Cnockaert in Roulers, Belgium in 1893 her espionage service was primarily in the first World War.

When the Germans overran Belgium in that war she used her job as a nurse in a German occupied hospital to get information. Employing the customary female cunning and wiles she managed to get information out of senior German officers which was relayed to Allied authorities.

She managed to retain her virtue although in her book, I WAS A SPY, she declared it was often precarious.

She detailed a common meeting place for transfer of espionage obtained material was the church.

"No celebration of divine service took place without a Secret Service agent being present", she said in her book. This applied to both sides and no doubt accounted for a higher than usual male presence at worship services. Finally her luck ran out and she was arrested. Tried as a spy by the Germans, she was found guilty and sentenced to death. The armistice saved her from that fate. She was mentioned by French Field-Marshal Earl Haig for 'gallant and distinguished services in the field.' Sir Winston Churchill wrote a foreword to her spy book. She died in 1969 with no word of what she did in WWII, if anything.

∧

XXI
Dr. Elsbeth Schragmuller

There were probably no more than two or three spy-mistresses during World War 11. One of these was Dr. Schragmuller, a patriotic German woman who sought a way to serve her country in a most unusual way. In 1913 she received her doctorate at Freiberg University. She then met and persuaded Colonel Nicolai to give her a position in the Nachrichtendienst which oversaw all German espionage.

Whether she was sent to Antwerp because of brilliant work or simply to get her out of Nicolai's hair, the fact was she was put in charge of a school that trained citizens to become spies. She ruled her students with an iron fist. Some described it as an almost sadistic severity.

At all times the students had to wear masks. They could be known as only numbers, no names. She would sometimes lock her charges in their rooms like little children. It was not unknown for them to often be punished by witholding dinner if their performance fell below her expectations. Her sharp, shrewd eyes won her the nickname among her students as 'Tiger Eyes.' Her philosophy was a spy could become a good spy simply by training. No natural talent was necessary.

But since the proof of a theory is in its actual performance it would seem she failed badly. Two of her pupils, Jenssen and Roos were sent on special missions to England. They were immediately exposed, tried and then shot.

In spite of it all she received high praise from Colonel Nicolai and others in the German command.

XXII
Maria De Victorica

The stereotype of a beautiful, seductive, blonde female spy was fulfilled by a mysterious German lady in 1917. Not only did she qualify because of her beauty but because she was a highly educated woman who spoke several languages. Her father was a well known German General.

The lady had served in German Naval intelligence in Russia, then went on to Chile where she married a man also involved in spying. American intelligence first became aware of her in November 1917.

The British advised a German agent had just left Madrid headed for New York and was carrying ten thousand dollars for someone there. They had only two names to offer. When agents checked them out they had already left so they left a stakeout and put an intercept on their mail. A letter came which gave no real information although the M18 Special Inks section said they did determine writing in secret ink between the lines.

A second letter came in. Though addressed to a man its content was for a woman. This time the secret writing between the lines was more legible—and incriminating. The recipient of the letter was already heavily involved in sabotage of American ships and war plants.

A return address on the envelope led them to a boardinghouse where a very nervous Norwegian sailor admitted to having mailed the letters. They were given to him by a friend in Oslo and were to be mailed when he reached America. He had switched them inadvertently when he reached New York. They had been put in his shoe and became quite dirty so he simply got new envelopes and readdressed them.

Could he recall who the woman was where the second letter went? He did and directed them to a woman in German Yorkville.

Yes, she remembered the letter but had thrown it out with other unsolicited letters that had come to her. (One of the ploys of German intelligence was to send letters to complete strangers, then rely on agents visiting and obtaining those letters.) Under continuous questioning all she could remember was one name—Victorica.

Whether it had meaning or not was another matter. It did not appear anywhere in American files. When the British and French were asked it was the British who said Victorica was a German woman wanted by them for political espionage. They had been looking for her since 1914.

Continued investigation revealed a woman fitting her description had passed through Customs in 1917 headed for New York. She was Maria de Victorica and had married a Chilean man named Victorica. Feeling their quarry was in New York City a full fledged search of first class hotels and apartments began.

She had just checked out of the Knickerbocker. She had also just checked out of the Waldorf Astoria, then several other hotels. In several cases she had made substantial payments of rent in advance.

The agents were baffled but British leads kept coming in. Finally a break came in the form of an intercepted cable. In it they learned a New York banking house had transferred $35,000 to her. They rushed to her address only to find she had once more disappeared. But they did find numerous letters which, when analyzed, revealed she was not only involved in sabotage but also the landing of arms in Mexico. Further she was involved other saboteurs including the infamous "Dynamite Charlie" Wunnenberg. Added to her operations was the duping of several Catholic priests•

Could they help her import some religious figures? Of course. In fact they were so taken they agreed to place the order in their names.

The religious figures contained 'Tetral' a powerful new explosive not unlike the plastic explosive of today.

But the mysterious beauty continued confounding them. Every possible lead was followed. Nothing came.

Sometimes a break comes out of the blue, when least expected. An agent watching a suspect observed a schoolgirl cousin as she went to St. Patrick's Cathedral on Fifth Avenue at the same time and on the same day each week. He reasoned it was not unusual for someone to go to church on the same day each week but at the same time seemed unusual.

It was dusk on the evening of April 16, 1918 when he tailed the girl to the church and watched as she knelt to pray, then rose. He was going to follow her out but noticed she had left a newspaper. He stood to pick it up but a well-dressed man now occupied the same pew carrying his own paper. He placed it on top of her paper, prayed and then left with both papers.

The agent tailed him to Pennsylvania Station where he boarded a train and got off at Long Beach. There he got into a cab and was taken to Hotel Nassau. For a long time the man sat in the lobby smoking his cigar and watching other people. He suddenly rose quickly and headed for the door. The agent rose to follow him but noticed he had left his newspapers and decided to pick them up.With split second timing, however, a blonde now occupied the same chair bringing her own newspapers which she placed on top of the others. She casually glanced through a magazine, then picked up all the papers and headed for the elevator.

Maria de Victorica spying days were over. She was immediately arrested with the incriminating paper containing over $20,000 from the German Minister to Mexico to finance her network. She was indicted by a Grand Jury but never faced her trial due to declining health. Due to the constant tension she was under she had a nervous breakdown. More importantly she had become a drug addict.Her former beauty a thing of the past, she was committed to Bellevue Hospital where she died in 1920.

∧

XXIII
Margaretha Gertrude Zelle Aka Mata Hari

Mention the term 'female spy' and you are bound to immediately hear reference to this woman. While the myth continues to expand regarding this legendary spy the truth is quite different. She was not beautiful, she was not exotic and as a dancer she was average at best.

What made her so famous during the first World War was the fact she danced nude. In her day this was so shocking as to make it world-wide news. It obviously drew all kinds of men of influence to her and thereby lies her tale.

She was born on August 7, 1876 in Leeuwarden Holland. Her father was a middleclass Dutchman who owned and ran a hat shop. At age 18 she met a 38 year old Dutch army Captain Campbell MacLeod, through an ad he had placed. Shortly after that they were married. Son Norman, quickly followed. They moved to Java in the West Indies where daughter, Jeanne Louise, was born. With their marriage deteriorating they moved back to Amsterdam in 1902 where her husband resigned his commission. It didn't help and a divorce followed.

She moved in with an uncle and soon met a man who ran a horse show. She applied for a job with the Cirque Molier horse show extravaganza telling of her riding prowess in Sumatra. She was hired and was a great success. The owner, however, impressed with her body and talent suggested she might do better as an exotic dancer. It would be necessary to create a whole new background—one flamboyant and mysterious.

Her Indies background provided just a touch of wickedness to titillate. And thus Maragaretha was born of parents involved as temple priests and all the trappings of the Indies. Her name became Mata Hari, "The Eye of the Dawn".

Her story was now that she was born in southern India to a family of sacred Brahmin caste. Her mother had died giving her birth. The temple priests of Kanda Swandy dedicated her to Siva and taught her temple dances. It was never revealed how she got to Paris.

She was twenty-nine when she began her new life. While not a beautiful woman she did have lovely eyes and arms that she used to their fullest. Her breasts were pendulous and flabby but she titillated with veils and her mysterious background. Millionaires and politicians stood in line. Jewels and money were showered on her and she was the toast of Paris.

But others began imitating her and she failed to vary her routine so her light began dimming. It was off to Berlin where she made new conquests. She demanded and got more and more money for her favors. Army officers found some of that money in funds marked for secret operations. This ensnared her in espionage for she picked up bits of information from Spanish, French, German, Italian, Swedish and Dutch clients—then passed them on.

There was no secrecy in her goings and comings between Paris and Berlin. She had no aptitude for espionage but did remember bits and pieces and freely passed them to her latest bed partner.

When World War I broke out she was left alone the first year. But in 1915 the Italian Secret Service alerted the French that this woman 'speaks German with a slight eastern accent.' It was the beginning of insinuating German sympathies.

Secret intelligence of other nations were advised of this and entered it in their files. The French tailed her but found nothing. They did learn that from her high placed clientele she had been privileged to send mail, uncensored, through their diplomatic pouches.

Dutch and Swedish officials opened their pouches and examined her letters and found nothing. But those actions played an important part in her trial.

She offered to serve in the French Secret Service and was accepted. She was sent to Belgium, then Scotland Yard and finally Spain where she teamed up with German Naval attache Captain Walter Canaris and two others. All of these men drew on the espionage fund to meet her price for special favors.

Germany weighed the price being paid for intelligence and the results and decided something was wrong. They soon realized the great bulk of the money was going to Mata Hari who was listed as a spy but actually was being paid for other talents.

Spies who lose their value are liquidated and this was to be the fate of Mata Hari. Captain Canaris (he later became head of all German Intelligence in World War II) was instructed to entrap her. Agent "H.21" was sent to Paris with a check for fifteen thousand pesates for 'services performed in Spain. She swallowed the bait and in Paris registered at the Hotel Plaza-Athenee in the

Avenue Montaigne. She never had time to cash the check as she was arrested 24 hours later.

She had sent a message to Captain Canaris in a code the Germans knew was known to the French. Though overt in nature the fact she used a German code would surely imply she was working for the Germans and betraying the French. Her liquidation would surely follow.

She was arrested and taken to cell No. 12 in the Saint-Lazare prison. Her trial began on July 24, 1917.

Her head held high she admitted to large sums of money from Germans as well as officials of other nations. The sums she freely admitted were for her special favors, nothing else. She brought as witnesses many of her high placed French clients but to no avail. The jury deliberated ten minutes. The sentence was death.

Her composure held and she showed no emotion at the verdict. And now myth and rumors began. One was that the Germans might make a desperate attempt to save her. Another was that high powers in the French government might intervene. Her 75 year old lawyer tried to invoke Article 27 of the French Penal code which stated a woman expecting to give birth could not be executed. He even implied he was the father (no doubt with a smile).

And one more story surfaced surrounding Pierre de Morrisac who was the younger son of a prominent French family. He had led a wild and degenerate life but had really fallen in love with Mata Hari. Taking a page from the opera, "Tosca", he planned a mock execution with blank cartridges for the firing squad. The plot was worked out in intricate detail and some feel could have counted for the calm way in which she had accepted her death verdict. It never came to pass. (In 1936 this same man faced a firing squad in Spain during the Spanish civil war).

The date was set for October 15, 1917 at 5:47. It was to be held at the Vincennes rifle range.That morning she accepted the glass of rum prescribed for the condemned by law, wrote three letters and said she was ready. A procession of cars took her to a square where troops waited on three sides. On the fourth side was a bare tree, stripped of all foliage and branches.

The death sentence was read and she was tied to the tree. The firing squad stood in position and waited the command of Major Massard. The shots rang out and she sank to the ground, her body pierced by twelve bullets.

"The Eye of the Dawn" was permanently closed.

Her daughter read, without tears, that last letter from her now deceased mother:

"My dear child:

There is much I would like to tell you and so little I can say. My time is getting short. Fading out. It is four in the morning and within an hour or so, I will be among the dead without ever having had the chance of seeing you again. You were a baby when I left you. Believe me, I did nothing that was wrong, but war has its own brutal laws. I do not believe in mercy for me, not even political friends can help me this time.

I had a good and full life. Perhaps it was not a happy one. Oh, we knew so little of each other, but Aunt Rose always sent me your report card, always told me what a fine and beautiful young woman you are. I had your picture.

I was young when I came to Bali and Java, too young to know, I fell in love with your father who started out as a fine man, but the tropics and the liquor, the death of our son, made him what he was. He almost killed me once. It was then I left him. Now others will kill me. I know I should have never deserted you. But perhaps a better life is ahead for you without me. I will die courageously, thinking of you. You were all I had and I did not take care of you. Money alone was not enough. Will you pray for me, will you remember me as a woman who wanted to do right? Life and circumstances were stronger than I. Goodbye my child, find your happiness in life and find it without hating me »

> Your mother,
> Maragaretha Gertrude Zelle-MacLeod

Her daughter read the letter and turned its contents over in her mind. Never in her wildest dreams could she have known she would also be executed as a spy for the C1A thirty-three years later in Korea.

XXIV
Marguerite Francillard

Her heart affluter, 18 year-old Marguerite Francillard was a dressmaker by trade in central France in 1915. Though not engaged in espionage herself she unwittingly caused great damage to France acting as a courier. She had fallen in love with a German who posed as a silk salesman and worked his way into her heart. As a courier she made numerous trips to Switzerland taking messages in and bringing others back to her lover. In 1916 she came under French surveillance and was arrested in Paris. At the time of her arrest she was carrying incriminating documents that sealed her fate.

The French incarcerated her in cell #12 of the Saint Lazare prison. This happened to be the same cell that had held the well known Mata Hari.

On January 10, 1917 Marguerite was executed.

XXV
Rose Daucimetiere

Romance also was the cause another young French girl became involved in espionage.

Nineteen year-old Rose Daucimetiere dined alone. Her waiter, Walter, was much more attentive than called for. Though he claimed to be Swiss he was actually German. He quickly dazzled the young girl and shortly she moved into his St. Martin apartment.

Willing to do anything for him she soon became a prostitute at his urging. Her clients were mainly French soldiers. Every day she would report to Walter what information she had received from the soldiers such as their units, where they had been and where they were going.

The information was relayed by Walter to the German High Command. In October 1916 Rose went to work in the Val de Grace Hospital as a nurse. She had now progressed to writing reports in invisible ink. A French censor detected them and she was arrested. At her trial she was condemned to death and returned to her cell. At the last minute French President Raymond Poincare reduced her sentence to life imprisonment where she eventually died.

The Spanish Civil War
XXVI
Angelica Dubrow Aka Helen Holborn

She filled the movie version of the attractive, svelte blonde as she boarded the Munich Express at the Anhalter Bahnhof in Berlin on June 10, 1935.

She changed to the Rome express when she reached Munich. She appeared aloof and read some magazines she had brought with her. An occasional man talked to her but was quickly rebuffed. The lady had no interest in male companionship.

Also seated in first class on the train was a Spaniard, Fernando Queseda. When his luggage was checked it revealed silk shirts and other trappings of a very well off gentleman. The train came to a stop in Rome and the passengers went their own way.

Angelica went to the Parkers Hotel in Naples and unpacked in her room. The next night she dressed in a pale blue suit, picked out a bouquet of white carnations and called for a cab. She told the driver to take her to the Zia Teresa restaurant in the port of Naples.

It was crowded when she arrived. She stood waiting for a table until a waiter saw the white carnations and approached her. "Unfortunately, madame, we have no table but if you wouldn't mind sharing a table.»».»»."

She was seated at a table with a lone man who welcomed her company. A few minutes later the Spaniard, Queseda, was led to their table. The three had never met but all knew of each other by reputation.

Angelica Dubrow was traveling under the name of Helen Holborn. She was a special agent in the Spanish

Section of the Gestapo and had earlier served the
Weimar Republic in a counterfeiting operation. Her
traveling companion on the train, Fernando Queseda,
had considerable experience in the field of espionage.
He brought with him one problem, however. It was
unwanted publicity including a newspaper photograph
of him and a story about bribery and gambling. He also
had been involved in smuggling cigarettes. The lone
gentlemen Angelica had first encountered was Gaston
d'Ette who represented Italy.

The German-Spanish-Italian trio was trying to
assemble a plan to put Franco in power in Spain, then
make that a Fascist state to join Germany and Italy.
Franco had been told the Spanish troops in Morocco
would be loyal to him. But it was not enough. The
answer, he felt, lay in air power. If he could get planes
from Germany and Italy he was assured of complete
power in Spain.

What he needed was eighty planes. Berlin and Rome
fell into line. The deal was sweetened by the fact Spanish
interests had agreed to pay for the planes.

The next problem was much more formidable: How
to get the planes to Morocco without attracting the
British and French, both hostile to Franco. The final
plan was to crate them and send them to Naples. There
they would be placed on smaller ships and sent to their
final destination.

The mounting enthusiasm was squelched by the
Spaniard. He advised that due to 'changed circumstances
the use of small ships for the final leg was out of the
question.

Asked to explain he said a mystery ship had been operating in the area of the small Moroccan ports in the area. The skipper was known only as Le Capitain Solitaire and it was felt he worked for the British Secret Service. His boat operated in waters barely navigable making it difficult to catch him. It was known secret radio messages were being sent from the area. No one could identify the Capitaine but it was known he had a bright, red beard.

After further analyzing the problem they felt a different port might solve the problem. They suggested Zuara in Libya, fifty miles west of Tripoli. The planes could be assembled there and flown to Morocco by night. Berlin and Rome concurred.

The Spaniard and Italian congratulated one another on the brilliant solution. But Angelica's intuition caused her to dig deeper into Le Capitaine.

"What do we know about him? We have to be on the watch," she opined.

Their information was skimpy at best. He sometimes was clean shaven but when he wasn't he had a bright red beard. His ship was seventy five feet in length with a diesel motor. It had no masts but did have funnel in back of a low bridge. It was a typical smugglers boat.

While they awaited the shipment of crates in Naples another drama had been played out in Emden, Germany, where the merchandise was being loaded.

No one on the pier paid any attention to a truck that drove up. A man in a light raincoat got out. He was sporting a hard hat and pair of gold rimmed glasses. There was a gap in his smile where an upper tooth was missing. From that gap protruded a long cigar. His paperwork was in order except for an additional crate he insisted be loaded aboard. The first mate disagreed and a loud conversation took place. Finally the stranger won, the crate was included .

Zaure had been strengthened militarily for the work that would be required when the crates arrived. Barbed wire and additional troops were to secure the area.

The three agents stood at the Zaure port as the crates arrived and were speedily loaded aboard trucks, then driven to the remote camp where mechanics and pilots awaited. The local Chief of Police made a call on the three one night. It was August 16, 1935. He brought a bottle of wine and they all drank toasts to one another.

Angelica brought it up. "Anything going on at the port?" she asked casually.

"Just a British fishing boat with some damage. Came in for repairs," he replied.

He was astounded by their reaction to the simple reply.

"How big is his boat?" was the next question.

"I'd say seventy five feet."

".»»..and the man?" Angelica demanded.

"Nice looking fellow»..has a reddish beard."

Noting their anxiety he said the boat really did have damage and if they'd like to see it he'd take them there.

When they arrived at the boat there was no one there. But there was no doubt it was Le Capitaine.

Suddenly the sky lit up and a thunderous explosion broke the silence» More explosions followed.

They drove furiously to the plant site and found the factory totally consumed by flames, those planes already assembled, destroyed.

The Police Chief returned to the boat and put two guards on it. They were instructed to shoot anyone who attempted to board it. Two weeks later two seasick Italian policemen reported to their Consul in Oran. Their tale was incredible.

They had been put aboard a small vessel with orders to let no one take it. Suddenly the boat took off with them aboard. The sea was rough and they were quite seasick. They feared their fate was to be dumped overboard. Instead they were put ashore at a lonely spot near Oran.

Somehow Le Capitaine had kept Franco from assuming power as early as 1935. The Italian agent, d'Ette, was exiled to the Lipari Islands where he committed suicide six months later. Angelica Dubrow was seen in Rio de Janeiro in 1938. She never bothered to return to Germany.

CHAPTER 4

▼

World War II

Governments were now taking women more seriously in their ever expanding role as intelligence agents. In the past they were often excused due to chivalry that excused them for many things a man would have been instantly imprisoned (or worse) for doing. Through macho eyes the women probably weren1't too guilty because, after all, how could they understand the severity of what she had done. And, if in possession of classified material, it most assuredly was beyond her comprehension so perhaps a severe lecture was all that was required•

In those early days it was too often a matter of fluttering eyelashes and wide eyed innocence that sufficed. In other cases it was also applying the worlds oldest profession to obtain information over a hot pillow.

Other countries had already realized the need to harness their women's unique abilities. In 1909 England established a civilian intelligence agency. Germany followed with its own branch in 1913 and Russia in 1917. France followed suit in 1935.

The United States officially formed the COI (Coordinator of Information) in July 1941 which became the OSS (Office of Strategic Services) in June 1942 and finally the C1A (Central Intelligence Agency) in 1945 after President Harry Truman had dissolved the OSS in August 1945.

During this great war there were three intelligence agencies that supervised allied resistance activities in Europe. These included the British Special Operations Executive, (SOE); the American OSS and the French Bureau Central de Reseignements et d'Action (BCRA) which was established in 1944 by General Charles de Gaulle.

It is estimated over 5,000 downed airmen were returned to their bases through the efforts of women who secreted them in their homes, fed and clothed them and finally supplied them with those documents necessary to go through enemy lines. Many men and women in operating these escape lines were arrested, deported, put in concentration camps or shot.

Approximately 50,000 people participated in the intelligence networks in Europe. Twenty percent of these were women. Many of them worked in the most dangerous areas—sabotage, paramilitary operations, teaching weaponry and codes.

Many of the women in Europe had no special training. They simply recognized what needed to be done and went about it.

· One thing now had become evident. The approach of an every day prostitute would fail in the high game of espionage. It appeared very few women, if any, could be detached enough not to betray themselves when doing this kind of work. They just cannot play on their sex without falling victims to its romance which they have started out only pretending to feel.

High ranking officers and officials are generally men of good character and virtue. A female spy would of necessity have to meet them on the same intellectual level which would be a difficult task unless she also has an exceptional background and intelligence—and is alluring. For that reason many sexy spies have failed.

OSS had over 21,000 military and civilian employees. Of these 4,002 were women who maintained the basic structure. General Donovan called them the "invisible apronstrings"• A small percentage of these women went overseas, a still smaller percentage actually served as secret agents.

The British used 10,000 men and 3,000 women in their spy operations. Fifty-three women were sent into France. Twelve were executed by the Nazis. Twenty nine were arrested or died in captivity. (A loss ratio of 78%). Before the war ended their area of service expanded into Egypt, Turkey and India. With typical British understatement their headquarters were listed simply as 64 Baker Street, London.

A new facet arose during WWII involving use of intelligence agencies. It revolved around the way enemy states might seek a feeling out of a proposal that was too sensitive to be approached through normal channels. It was more simple to propose it to an OSS or CIA agent to see how his government might feel about it. In turn the agent then relays it to his government and some negotiations might then begin that later could develop into full fledged negotations at the highest level.

One such example was a suggestion through the Gestapo to the OSS (hardly soulmates) in 1945 that Germany might consider a double cross of Japan. They would turn over all intelligence they had regarding Japanese navy, ground and air forces. In turn America would hold up its western front allowing Germany to deal a final fatal blow to Russia. Indeed if American forces would join German troops to defeat Russia then Germany would help the Allies defeat Japan•

This classic double cross came through the OSS Switzerland headquarters and received the scant attention it deserved. It did show, however, that there is yet another service our intelligence service does provide.

OSS Structure

The seemingly unstructured OSS organization was anything but that. With a genius toward organizing the security, recruiting, training, medical services, special funds, photographic and communications operations under which the men and women operated the following were established:

Research and Analysis (R&A) To produce the economic, military, social and political studies and estimates for every strategic area from Europe to the Far East.

Secret Intelligence (SI) to gather on-the-spot information from within neutral and enemy territory.

Special Operations (SO) To conduct sabotage and work with resistance forces.

Counterespionage (X-2) To protect our own and Allied intelligence operations, and—to identify enemy agents overseas.

Operational Groups (OG) To train and supply and lead guerrilla forces in enemy territory.

Maritime Unit (MU) To conduct maritime sabotage.

Schools and Training (S&T) In overall charge of the assessment and training of personnel, both in the United States and overseas.

Women operated in every one of these divisions with the exception of the Maritime Unit. They had no problems in accepting the discipline and guidelines they worked under. Secrecy was maintained within each of the groups. It was said that Donovan himself did not know, or want to know, the names of some of the most successful agents. Other branches could only get information on a "need to know" basis. The overall departmentalization was overwhelmingly successful.

Research and Analysis

A most important area of female service lay in the Research & Analysis division of OSS. Donovan had said, "Our experience showed that a half hour spent with a brakeman of a freight train running in occupied France would produce more useful information than a Mata Hari could learn in a year…the major part of our intelligence was the result of good old-fashioned intellectual sweat."

Based on that principle R&A provided probably the greatest bulk of intelligence information by pouring over foreign newspapers, obscure technical journals, from reports of international business firms and labor organizations. Taking the many assembled facts they fit them into a giant mosaic of raw material and strategy.

The natural curiosity of women entered into the sometimes boring search through printed pages of material looking for the smallest detail that might be of interest. With patience and a natural affinity for spotting the most minute details they contributed to the emerging jigsaw puzzle being assembled daily.

Scientist Dr. Langer of R&A stated, "Back in 1944, John Gardner, later head of the Carnegie Foundation and Jim Perkins, president of Cornell expressed their opinion that R&A had pioneered an important new direction in education. After the war the Carnegie Foundation put up the initial money to start Russian and Middle East and Far East Research Centers at Harvard, Columbia and elsewhere, with sociologists and political scientists and historians all working on the same area study—a very important part of the modern university curriculum." The original R&A unit was established in 1941 and was listed as a part of the Library of Congress. It included scholars drawn from the social science fields—economists, historians, geographers, psychologists, archaeologists, anthropologists and philologists.

(footnote)

"It is a curious fact of academic history that the first great center of area studies in the United States was not located in any university, but in Washington during the Second World War, in the Office of Strategic Services. In very large measure the area study programs developed in American universities in the years after the war were manned, directed or stimulated by graduates of the OSS-a remarkable institution, half cops-and-robbers and half faculty meeting. It is still true today, and I hope it will always be, that there is a high measure of inter-penetration between universities with area programs and information-gathering agencies of the government of the United States." McGeorge Bundy in The Dimensions of Diplomacy, edited by E.A.J. Johnson (Baltimore, 1964)

The multi-talented staff of advisers was credited with the production of the most accurate estimates made by the Allies in World War II.

XXVII
MARTHA RICHER AKA THE LARK

She derived her name from her fellow Frenchman because she was an aviatrix. Her male companions used the French word, "L'Alouette" which translated in English was 'lark'.

It was during World War 1 her husband was killed. He was a French officer fighting the Germans. Whether out of revenge or patriotism is not clear but Martha decided to serve her nation in her own way.

She went to Captain Georges Ladoux who headed French military intelligence. To test her he assigned her to work on the German colony at San Sebastian in Spain.

There she met Dr. Stephan who was an Abwehr agent. He suggested she spy for the Germans to which she agreed...except there was to be one provision. She must meet Capatain Hans von Krohn who headed German espionage in Spain.

She was an extremely attractive woman and spoke several languages making her highly desireable as an agent to say nothing of a close personal relationship.

As she anticipated she soon became his mistress. He assigned her the task of getting production figures of the Schneider armaments combine in Paris.

When she reached that city she promptly reported to French intelligence who were only too glad to provide her with fake figures to feed the Germans. They worked and the Germans were entirely taken in.

So impressed with her performance was von Krohn he ordered her to act as a courier to Buenos Aires. She departed with highly secret material for Germans in that country. In addition she was given a suitcase containing vials with enough chemicals to "destroy the whole of the Allies wheat stock in South America."

Aboard the ship she made her final decision. One night she went on deck and first threw the suitcase with the chemicals overboard. Then two more trips followed when she also threw all the secret material for the German agents. She was making her break final. Von Krohn never learned of her action before the war ended. When it did she confessed to her former lover that she had been a double agent all along. Then she left.

His final comments are not known—but they were no doubt unprintable anyway.

XXVIII
Micheline Mathilde Carre aka the Cat

Intelligence can be a game to some—played on both sides of the court and for reasons unfathomable to many. There are those who simply work for the highest bidder, others who for ego purposes like to prove they can fool both sides.

The reasoning of Micheline Carre still is not clear. She served both the French and the Germans quite well. It concluded with her trial and conviction on January 8, 1949. She was then forty years old.

First recorded evidence of her was in 1939 in southern Algeria. Her husband was a French army officer. His pay was so low she had to take a job as a schoolteacher to make ends meet. She was described as extremely attractive and an elegant appearance in spite of poor financial circumstances.

With the outbreak of World War II she set out for Paris, anxious to leave Algeria. She took a job as a nurse. Her husband had been killed in battle.

She did something a spy should never do—kept a diary. But at the outset she had no idea she would become involved in this line of work.

She fell in love with Paris. Loved to walk its streets, look at the people, the sidewalk cafes, the museums and the theatre. The onslaught of the German army sent her first to Beauvais, then Toulouse.

She brought some order out of the confusion surrounding retreating soldiers and misplaced civilians. She organized an assembly center for the wounded and to help soldiers detached from their units find where they belonged.

At this point she met a Polish general staff officer who had been acting as liaison with the French. He was in poor health. She nursed him back to health. His name was Roman Czerniawski which was too hard to prounounce. She called him Armand. He called her The Cat because of her feline grace. They quickly became lovers.

Their relation expanded when he told her his plan was to organize an espionage unit to work against the Germans. She gladly joined him. Their group was called Interallie and soon became one of the most active. Colonel Marcel Achard also came aboard. He was most important as he had contacts through Spain and Portugal with the British.

Their group added French aristocrat, Pierre de Vomecourt. Their work included arranging air drops, delivery of supplies by ships along the coast, hiding deserters and smuggling people over the Swiss border.

A French woman, Renee Borni joined them causing a jealous rift between Carre and her lover—but not a serious one. Borni was given the name of Violette for resistance work purposes. Achard pointed out a huge problem existed over whether or not the Germans would march into and through Spain and take Gibraltar. The cat was sent to Biarritz where she found an S.S. tank unit that seemed to be preparing for such an invasion. Nearby there were air units assembling.

At a cafe she was approached by a German officer. She found out he was one in command of all supplies for the Luftwaffe in the Bordeaux area.

Additional investigations by The Cat convinced her the Germans were preparing for the Spanish invasion. She so reported it. Told to hang around longer, she did. The units began pulling back convincing her the Germans were not going to invade. She reported this and it proved correct. The Germans had given up the idea.

Violette, attempting to gain some information on a specific German unit, questioned a German Sergeant. A man sitting nearby was listening in and followed her as she left. She was unaware of her surveillance for several days. During this time she had been seen with The Cat and Armand.

On November 18, 1941, Violette and Armand were arrested. Soon thereafter The Cat was picked up.

Her interrogator was a German sergeant, Hugo Bleicher. She evidently became his mistress the first night. Unexplainably she led the Germans to thirty five of the top French resistance workers, all of whom were arrested. She never did betray Armand. She learned that Violette had been working with the Germans all along.

So many resistance workers were arrested, she informed the Germans, they could no longer communicate with England. The Germans decided on a bold move. She would have to go to England, together with Vomecourt. Through German connivance they were able to get into England.

There, incredibly, the two went to work for the War Office in London. They sent information to Violette who relayed it to Bleicher.

British intelligence had been taking a long, hard view at The Cat and Vomecourt. They were arrested in July, 1942. She was incarcerated in England for the duration of the war.

Upon returning to France she faced trial for the lives of the brave resistance workers she had betrayed. On January 8, 1949, she was sentenced to death. It was changed to life imprisonment a few months later by the French President. She now sits silently in her cell with ample time to recall those she betrayed.

XXIX
Jeanette

In a continuing display of the cunning female mind, to say nothing of courage and bravery, a French housewife and mother of two named Jeanette volunteered for OSS missions behind enemy lines.

An agent was needed near the Vosge mountains. Would she go? There was no hesitation as she got her instructions, drew her equipment and dropped behind the lines for a third mission.

She was warmly greeted by the resistance forces. Unfortunately, among them was a German sympathizer who betrayed her. She was tortured for a week but revealed nothing. They decided she needed the more advanced tortures only the Gestapo could inflict and she was awaiting transfer to one of their prisons. Her mind was at work constantly looking for that one advantage. It came in the form of the guard who brought her food each day. Her cell had a heavy iron door which the guard would violently throw open with his shoulder. She began her plan.

One day she secreted a shard of glass and cut her scalp causing it to bleed violently. They she lay on the floor, her head pointed toward the door. After flinging the door open in his usual manner he discovered the bleeding prisoner and had her 'unconscious' body taken to the hospital. From there it was easier to escape which she did. She made her way back to Allied lines. As soon as her scalp healed she immediately volunteered for another mission.

XXX
The Unknown Heroine of Peenemunde

The second unnamed female was responsible for the delay of the V-l bomb attacks on England. She was working in the Germans main research station at Peenemunde on the Baltic in 1942. The British were aware of secret German operations relating to the planned 'horror weapon', the V-l bomb. In some manner she got information to them for the bombing of that facility at a most devastating time for the Germans. The bombers that blasted the facility hit at the exact time many of the scientists representing the war potential of Germany were visiting. After the bombers left the Germans found two hundred of the top scientists were killed along with General Hans Jaschonnek, Luftwaffe Chief of Staff.

It was one of the most damaging bomb attacks of the war. Infuriated, the Gestapo sealed off the island and questioned every person. They were ordered to find the source of leakage. In searching the bodies of the dead they found one girl with a London bus ticket in her pocket. Records indicated she had been recommended by a high Nazi official. On that basis the Germans decided the ticket was simply evidence of a peacetime visit to England and dismissed it.

If the most efficient Germans had pursued it they would have discovered the ticket was printed on wartime paper. They had found the spy they were seeking but never knew it. This also unnamed woman died in the raid she had brought down on her own head. She died alone and unmourned.

XXXI
The Unknown Lady Known Only As 'La Sourist (The Mouse)

It is difficult to assess what were the most singular achievements of agents, male or female, during World War II. Certainly two had to be those of women who remain nameless even to today in the files of London, Paris and Washington. The first was named The Mouse due to her unique scratching on doors and windows, Her secret signal.

She worked for the Vichy government as a civil servant. In this capacity she met a French technician who was working for the Germans under extreme coercion. He slipped her blueprints of the then planned V-l flying bomb. He only knew she had some sort of connection with the resistance and in desperation hoped she could get the blueprint to the British or Americans. She carefully weighed all options. Who could she trust with such vital papers?

Finally, she reached a decision and made arrangements to meet a courier whose credentials seemed sound enough. She was convinced he could smuggle them out of France, into London.

The day she was to see him with the blue prints she was unavoidably detained and arrived five minutes late. As she reached their rendezvous point she saw him being led away by the Germans. The fact she was late saved her and the plans. Quickly she made other arrangements. This time it was successful. The R.A.F. and U.S. Air Corps were supplied vital clues enabling them to set up such defenses as possible.

XXXII
The Marquisard Traffic Director

The French Maquis had many women serving in dangerous and important ways. They were too numerous to be identified except in their own local villages. Some became so proficient they won the respect of all resistance workers. In some cases men willingly took orders from young women. As long as it was for their cause the gender and age barriers were ignored.

As an example A nameless young Maquisard stood at a road junction during a German retreat and calmly misdirected a German battalion into an Allied trap

XXXIII
Madame Andree Goubilion

She managed a small cafe in Paris during the occupation. Her husband was imprisoned by the Germans. She let her cafe become a permanent letter drop for OSS, fed and sheltered no less than twenty one OSS agents and hid their wireless transmitter sets in her cellar. For any one of these activities she surely would have received the death sentence.

XXXIV
The Marchesa

Sounding like a television movie, a widowed Italian Marchessa, also served. The aristocratic lady had an ancestral palazzo in southern Italy which was taken over by the Germans for a communication center. She was permitted to live in one small wing of her home. Her hump-backed gardener, actually an OSS agent, was allowed past the sentries at the gate. He installed a small induction microphone with a threadlike wire powerful enough to pick up enemy conversations in the adjoining rooms as well as monitoring messages to forward German operational posts. Hobbling along at regular intervals the gardener returned to pick up the intelligence the Marchesa had acquired and forwarded it to OSS headquarters. When the Allies landed at Salerno her house became the central point for the entire German communication system.

She sent word to the 15th Air Force of the German activity and that their command post must be destroyed. She piled her personal belongings in a donkey cart and drove past the German sentries into town. The next morning Liberator bombers from Sicily blew her home to bits.

XXXV
Gertrude Legendre

The first American woman to be captured by the Germans was Gertrude Legendre, a big game hunter and sportswoman. Her capture greatly concerned OSS because she had been in the message center in London prior to being transferred to Paris. Here she sought adventure and on a short leave she talked two other OSS men into a trip to the front lines near Luxembourg. They subsequently came under fire where both of the men were wounded. All three were taken into

German headquarters. Before they surrendered she was able to hide incriminating documents but one of the men failed to do so and was identified as an OSS officer.

They were separated and she was questioned severely about her background. She stuck to her story that she was merely a clerk and had no idea of what was going on in the office. A German officer was gentle in his approach and advised he had run a small café in America. He had returned to Germany to pick up his wife and while there the war broke out and he was trapped. He managed to keep her in his Wehrmacht operation and shielded her from the Gestapo.

As the battle lines changed she was shifted back and forth in cars and the train. As the train neared the Swiss border she slipped off and ran across the border tofreedom.

OSS was not anxious to jeopardize other American prisoners and made no mention of her capture and escape.

After the war ended she ran down the German officer who was living with his family in near poverty.He was brought to America and for awhile worked for her husband.

She continued in government service working for the CIA. Her job included laying plans to be implemented if the Soviets attacked Europe.

XXXVI
Peggy Taylor Aka Suzanne

In June 1994 I was guest lecturer on the Crown Odyssey out of London. It was a cruise commemorating the 50th anniversary of D-Day at Normandy on June 6, 1944.

Among the mostly WWII veteran passengers was a tall, elegant white haired lady. Only after someone else told me did 1 learn she was a decorated veteran of

French intelligence with over 22 jumps behind enemy lines to her credit.

Her name was Peggy Taylor and in her soft-spoken voice this gentle English lady told me of her many missions in enemy territory. Though her parents were English she was born and raised in France. When the war broke out she and her siblings escaped to England. They later returned to France to fight the Germans.

Her assassination of a Gestapo Colonel violated one basic rule of intelligence operations. Missions of a personal nature against the enemy should not be carried out by agents with a personal vendetta. In such a situation the desire for revenge might cloud one's perspective and result in tragedy. Peggy Taylor had that reason—her mother, she had been informed, was in a concentration camp. Her arrest had triggered a fatal heart attack in Peggy's grandmother.

Fortunately the incident went smoothly (except for the Colonel) and she pulled it off. Living alone in a Veterans home now we keep in touch by phone regularly.

The lonely coastal road in the Normandy region of France was peaceful and quiet in March 1944. It was a gloomy day, the birds flew low, squawking as they went. A light breeze threatened to bring a storm that was forming to the north.

An occasional car drove by as well as some German armored cars moving from outpost to outpost for inspection of their defenses against a pending Allied invasion.

Several bicyclists moved slowly going about their business. One of them was 22 year old Peggy Taylor. Her dress and manner were those of a prostitute. She stopped everywhere she could engage a German soldier in conversation, flirted outrageously and, if no invitation to rendezvous, moved on. But her keen eyes had picked up the emblem identifying the soldiers unit which was what she really sought.

Peggy Taylor was a member of French Intelligence who had worked with the resistance and now was on a special mission under auspices of the American OSS. A month earlier she had met with Generals Eisenhower and DeGaulle in London. Impressed with her past service they asked her to bicycle the entire Normandy coast and identify as many military units as possible. She had long played the game and required no special instructions about being too curious or keeping incriminating notes.

When an officer of sufficient rank did proposition her she would have to carry through with her alleged prostitute role. Her mission was one that could only be entrusted to someone who knew the game well. If caught she might, under torture, reveal her instructions to work the Normandy Coast—a sure tip-off to the Germans.

Prior to this mission and afterwards she made a total of 22 jumps behind enemy lines to carry out espionage and sabotage. The last six jumps were made in a party dress, barefoot with her high heels tied around her neck.

When she landed she immediately put on her shoes and set out. If her welcoming committee was not on hand and the Germans, alerted by the low flying plane she had just exited came upon her, she had an explanation.

"Yes, 1 heard the plane but 1 have seen nothing. As you can see *I'm* on my way to (or from) a party".

She did carry a pistol in her purse but realized the folly of having to shoot it out with a German patrol. This she would have done preferring death to capture and torture.

Peggy had just barely escaped from the German invasion with her brothers at the outbreak of WWII. After a hazardous boat trip across the English channel they settled down in England. Her mother elected to remain behind with her own mother, seriously ill with a heart condition.

She and her brothers found her father who worked for the Forestry Service. Her 16 year-old brother tried to join the Free French Forces but was two years shy. Peggy forged her father's signature gaining him entrance but with a proviso—he was to find out where women might join. He agreed. In 1942 on her 21st birthday she joined the Bureau Centrale de Renseignment et d'Action, the French Underground. She had a special incentive. The Red Cross informed her that her grandmother had died from a heart attack—the result of seeing her daughter, Peggy's mother, arrested by the Germans and put in a concentration camp.

Her training came in a British camp for women where she learned firearms, demolition, communications, parachute jumping and intelligence gathering.

Her first assignment was to go into a local town to gather sensitive information. If she passed she would be sent into France. What they did not tell her was they had given her picture to the police and told them she was a prostitute dealing in drugs and should be arrested. She got the information without being arrested and was sent into France with no further delay.

Her first jump was just outside Paris where a man she knew only as 'the General' met her. They went into a bar for drinks. A man in civilian clothes looked over and said, "I'm with the Gestapo." She was puzzled. Then he moved in asking her to join him at his apartment just across the street for some drinks. The General nudged her and said softly, "yes, yes, yes." She agreed.

In the general conversation Suzanne (the name she was going under) asked him what time he went to work in the morning and if he had his own car. He told her had his own car and left about 8:00 a.m. At this point the General said, "Sweetheart, we've got to be going."

Suzanne replied, "Yes, darling. We've taken up too much of this man's time."

They agreed to meet him the next night and departed. When they reached the street the General thanked her for finding out when he left and said some of his men would 'take care of him' the next morning. Suzanne, now Peggy, replied she would do it herself.

"That's a man's job," the General replied.

"So is parachuting and I do that. Look," she said opening her handbag to reveal her gun. Then she said she wanted to do it to avenge her mother now in a concentration camp. He agreed.

The next morning the German came out in his Gestapo uniform. He was shocked to see Peggy approach him, gun in hand. She wasted no time in shooting him, then fled the scene.

The radio that night reported the assassination of a Gestapo Colonel but said they had no clues.

On one of her many return trips to London a new assignment awaited her. A known German spy was turned over to her with instructions to wine and dine him and see what she could learn about his other contacts. She was to take him to the bar of the Ritz at St. James Street, have lunch with him at the officers' mess and in general flirt with him. Then she was to take him to her room which they had reserved for her in Soho.

After climbing the three flights to her apartment they entered. Those who had arranged for her apartment had left the lights on which the German thought odd.

Feeling the event was turning sour she removed her pistol, put it in his back and said, "Okay, you dirty German. Don't move or I'll shoot."

He said, "You know I'm German. how?"

"1 knew it when we first met".

'Oh, Peggy, I was going to ask you to marry me".

"Too bad. Now walk or I'll shoot."

She prodded him into the living room where two British Military Police arrested him. She was later told he identified five other German agents. The British took all six outside London and executed them.

In September 1944 her mother was repatriated from the Concentration Camp. She had been badly treated, her health broken.

After the war Peggy was sent to Austria to work with occupation authorities. In May 1948 she went to Prague to pick up some fake ID documents and money. They were keeping an eye on the Communists within that country. Two days later the Russian army invaded Czechoslovakia. She needed to return to Austria so all her secret documents were sewn into the lining of her tunic. At the border the Russians went through her purse and luggage. She sat in her seat feeling the documents concealed in the lining behind her back. They were distracted by some aspirin tablets. "Cocaine", they shouted.

"No, aspirin", she replied.

"No, cocaine," they insisted. They left and happily did not return.

Her last official mission came in 1949. She and a British Colonel were to go into Yugoslavia and bring out the family of a government official who had fled. Driving into the country with forged papers they found the wife and three young children. They talked their way back through Russian checkpoints and all got out safely. Later in a plane crash she suffered a broken back and did not walk for several years. Now, retired, she lives at a Veterans Home in Canada.

CHAPTER 5

▼

XXXVII
Aline Griffith, The Countess De Romanones

I met the Countess in 1988 when we appeared jointly on KABC-TV in Los Angeles. She was on a tour promoting her first book, THE SPY WORE RED, which told of her actions as an OSS agent in Madrid. Local talk show hostess, Stephanie Edwards, had a program, Mid-Morning L.A. and I, as a former agent, was also invited to join the two ladies.

We first met after our makeup when we were on our way into the studio. All female spies are alleged to be gorgeous. She definitely qualified in addition to being articulate and witty. Walking onto the set we both admitted we had checked up on each other to verify authenticity. It struck us as funny and we approached our hostess laughing out loud. Stephanie found it surprising there would be such light heartedness and humor in agents but entered into the spirit and we had a great program.

Aline and 1 found we both had had some of the same
trainers in our OSS school. We both spoke French so she
was sent to Spain. I went to Burma.

C'es t la guerre.

Over the years 1 have read her two other books,
THE SPY WENT DANCING and THE SPY WORE
SILK, both best sellers. She is an extraordinary woman
as you will see.

The beautiful spy theme advanced in countless stories, both fiction and nonfiction, became a reality with
this special woman. Born in 1923 in Pearl River, New
York, Aline Griffith became one of the better known
women in the world. After graduating from College she
decided to become a Hattie Carnegie model but longed
for adventure. World War II was raging. Her brothers
were both serving and she longed to get involved also.

One night at a party she spoke of her desire to do
something overseas for the war effort. The man she
talked to asked a few questions, then asked for her phone
number. She thought it was just the typical case of an
older man (he was in his early 3Os) wanting the phone
of a younger woman. Nevertheless she gave it to him.

A few days later she received a call and was asked to
come to a certain building for an interview. The organization was the OSS and she answered the questions correctly. Her next instructions were more exciting than she
could have bargained for.

"Can you leave for Washington, D.C. within ten
days..if all goes well you will not return...give this phone
number to your parents where a message can be left for
you.•»».bring clothing suitable for the country.»••carry
nothing with your initials or letters with your

name.»..no one must be able to identify anything about you…go directly to Q building…give a false name and address to the receptionist…any questions?"

She had none.

Soon she was enrolled in the secret OSS training camp known as 'the Farm', just outside Washington, D.C. Together with other recruits they were all asked to take code names and reveal nothing of themselves. Each night they were encouraged to tell on each other—whose initials they might have picked up; where he or she came from; languages spoken; foreign ties or special talents.

Figuring she was one of the youngest and certainly with no special skills, 'Tiger', (her codename) felt she would be one of the first to drop out. To her surprise she made it.

After completing her training she was sent overseas to Portugal. Her first night in Lisbon brought her in contact with death. In a casino a man was stabbed to death, his lifeless body lying on the floor. As a neutral city Lisbon was a hotbed of international espionage as belligerents from both sides frequented its night spots and cafes.

Aline and her escort, a fellow agent, rushed to the scene after a woman's scream. A heavyset man was lying face down, a knife protruding from his back. When he was pronounced dead her companion said they could not get involved, they must leave immediately. It led Aline to wonder if he knew the man.

The next day another agent commented about some OSS problems including one of their own who had been murdered the night before. She had a quick introduction into the field of violence and treachery.

Her destination was the Standard Oil Company, in Madrid, an OSS front. Performing cryptography at first it was soon obvious her talents lay in espionage against a very well entrenched German intelligence operation. The Gestapo used some very beautiful German women who appeared at top social functions.

Aline became the OSS counterpart as she also was taken to the parties to seek information. Her main duty was to protect the planned invasion of southern France, operation ANVIL. She was instructed to learn what she could of what the Germans might know—or suspect.

The game turned rough one night when a Gestapo agent tried to strangle her in a car. She removed her .25 caliber pistol, shot him and fled. Returning to her apartment she contacted her superior who went out to take care of things. She was never told if he was dead or not. She thinks he was but that they wanted to spare her feelings over such a tragic encounter.

She was invited to numerous weekend parties at villas and castles. One weekend she loaned her apartment to two Basque women who had come down from the Pyrenees mountains with information on German troop movements. When she returned to her apartment on Monday she found the woman sleeping in her bed dead, shot through the head. Aline's good timing was bad timing for the Basque woman.

A major German radio was uncovered by Aline along with one of the top German agents in Madrid.

She remained active after OSS was disbanded in August 1945. In 1947 she married a Spanish Count she had met during the war. He was the Count of Quintanilla. Later through the Spanish process of succession the name was changed to de Romanones thus making her the Countess de Romanones.

Her OSS experiences were detailed in the first of her three best-seller books, 'THE SPY WORE RED'. She continued her exciting lifestyle after marriage by doing undercover work to discover a mole in the United Nations. A second book, 'THE SPY WENT DANCING1 told of those operations. A third book, 'THE SPY WORE SILK1 covered operations in Morocco together with former OSS agent, then CIA Director, Bill Casey.

XXXVIII
Julia McWilliams Child

Though Julia Child and her husband, Paul, both served in the CBI theater for OSS as I did, I met her there only once. She was in OSS DET 404 which operated out of Ceylon (now Sri Lanka). Her unit coordinated operations through the Bay of Bengal, the coast of Burma and as far east as Siam. One of their first missions was a dangerous and arduous reconaissiance of Simalur Island off the west coast of Sumatra.

Operation NOAH came across her desk several times. It was a daring plan to capture a Chinese junk and substitute a trained OSS crew. It would then sail up and down the Malayan coast of the Malacca Straits collecting intelligence and organizing cells for the penetration of Singapore. The junk was captured and operated for several months before intense Japanese surveillance caused the project to be abandoned.

In Siam they oversaw contact with the Regent of Siam, Luang Pradit.

Julia, a civilian, served as head of the Registry of the Secretary, OSS. She registered and catalogued vast volumes of documents. Thes were extremely sensitive, not only due to secrecy of operations, but also politically. OSS worked with British approval and it was incumbent on us not to embarrass the U.S. Government by stirring up dissension between the two countries. Any show of support for the Siamese against the British, who controlled the country politically, would create huge problems.

And yet OSS realized their best ploy was to hold out hope of American help to Siam in her struggle to maintain her independence and territorial integrity against suspected British designs. Julia's files contained the intrigue that went into these negotiations. Through it all she was noted for her accuracy and cheerfulness which raised the morale of her unit. This was noted when she was awarded the Emblem of Meritorious Civilian Service by her superiors. And through it all—she couldn't even make coffee.

She wrote a foreword for my book, THIS GRIM AND SAVAGE GAME, that stated, "My husband, Paul, and I served with the OSS from 1943 until the bomb was dropped. We were first in Washington, D.C. Then we went to New Delhi and finally on to Ceylon. I, myself, was always in the files—though I had hoped to become a spy, thinking that my six-foot height would be a good cover-up! It was a most stimulating and interesting time in our lives, and we all felt we were saving the world."

XXXIX
Betty McIntosh—Marjorie Severyns

Corporal Ishi Tagahaki trotted slowly down the jungle trail. The heavy foliage of North Burma hid the numerous animals whose sounds revealed they were all about.

Tagahaki was attached to the Japanese 18th Division occupying Burma during World War 11. He was at this moment a courier bearing his pouch of messages and communications to the area commanders. He had left the Japanese bastion of Myitkyina and was within two miles of his goal when a bullet dropped him on the narrow trail. A native stepped from behind the heavy brush and first made sure he was dead. Then the native opened his dispatch bag and inserted a document, resealed it and silently slipped back into the jungle.

The death of the lone soldier was part of a plan masterminded by a team in New Delhi. It included a Japanese scholar, a Japanese prisoner of war and research analysts, Betty McIntosh and Marjorie Severyns (Ravenholt) of OSS. They had been advised of a change of command at the top level in Tokyo. New people had been put in charge. The two women and others in their group wondered just how OSS might take advantage of the new situation.

The Japanese soldier, they knew, was trained from infancy that he must fight to the death. Surrender was out of the question if he wanted to go to the national shrine of Yasukuni. To change his mind would be impossible. But, knowing he would obey orders from his superior without question, she began thinking. In some way a new direction must seemingly come from Tokyo telling the soldiers that surrender was permissible under certain circumstances. What would be the circumstances» she pondered. And how could the forged OSS message be made to look authentic?

Together with a Japanese scholar they worked on the first problem. The soldiers were to be told that surrender was not dishonorable if he was seriously ill, vastly outnumbered or low on ammunition or supplies. If this could be made to look official and distributed to Japanese forces it could greatly lessen the fighting and save lives on both sides.

But the bigger problem remained of how to present it in such a way it would be accepted as a new policy of the Japanese government. The women aided by OSS agent, and Japanese scholar, Bill Magistretti, refined the wording. The same quality of rice paper was needed along with the proper dyes to forge the official chop.

There was a Japanese POW who was not sympathetic to the war but would never turn traitor to his home country. Magistretti was sent to talk with him. He was sullen and uncommunicative. Suddenly he studied Magistertti's face, then smiled. He reached out to shake his hand

'Otomodashi', (friend) he said.

It turned out the two had been good friends as they studied together at Waseda Ukniversity. He readily agreed to help in order to shorten the war.

The document was formulated, proper forgeries applied and it was ready .

Then it was necessary to learn of the Japanese courier system that took messages from the main bastion in the north to commanders in the area.

Captured Japanese documents were analyzed until they felt they could indeed create a believable document. Somehow that document must be put with other bona fide documents to be accepted. It was then they decided the lone courier who ran the messages into the jungle outposts was the key. The doctored document must somehow get into his pouch. The final solution was decided.

After killing the courier the native ran to the nearest Japanese outpost. He reported he had come across the body of a Japanese soldier on the trail and agreed to take a small patrol to retrieve it.

With the body safely in their camp the Japanese removed the pouch and retrieved the documents. As McIntosh, Severyns and Magilstretti had thought, the document was accepted as official policy of the new government. It was distributed through the area.

Suddenly Japanese began surrendering for the first time. An entire village fell without a fight as the Japanese decided they were hopelessly outnumbered or too ill to continue fighting. Quite a few feigned unconsciousness. Stockades which heretofore contained very few prisoners were crowded.

McIntosh, Severyns and Magisgtretti received no medals for their contribution to the war effort. There was no way to guess the number of lives saved. Quietly and effectively, however, they had contributed greatly to the war effort.

XL
Velvalee Dickinson

The story began in a doll shop in New York City and a returned letter.

The letter was in the possession of a Mary Wallace and greatly puzzled her. It had been sent to Argentina and was returned with the notation, "Moved. Left no forwarding address. Return to sender."

Mary Wallace knew no one in Argentina and opened the envelope to see just what was going on. It was typewritten and signed with her name. Further annoying was the fact it contained many misspellings and grammatical errors. She read:

Dear friend:

you probably wonder what has become of me as I havent written to you for so long. We have had a pretty bad month or so. My little nephew the one 1 adore so has a malignant tumor on the brain and isnt expected to live, so we're all crushed that we dont know what we are doing. They are giving him exray on the head and they hope to check it but give us absolutely no hope in a complete cure and maybe not even any relief. I am completely crushed. You asked me to tell you about my collection a month ago. I had to give a talk to an Art Club so I talked about my dolls and figurines. The only new dolls 1 have are those lovely Irish dolls. One of these three dolls is an old Irish Fisherman with a net over his back another is an old woman with wood on her back and the third is a little boy.

Everyone seemed to enjoy my talk 1 can only think of our sick boy these days.

You wrote me that you had sent a letter to Mr. Shaw he destroyed your letter, you know he has been ill. His car was damaged but is being repaired now. I saw a few of his family about. They all say Mr. Shaw will be back to work soon. I do hope my letter is not too sad. There is not much 1 can to write you these days.

I came in this short trip for Mother on business before I make out her income tax report that is also WHY 1 am learning to type. Everyone seems busy; these days the streets are full of people. Remember me to your family sorry I havent written to you for long. Truly

Mary Wallace

PS mother wanted to go to Louville but due to our worry the Louville plan put out our minds now.

Making the matter more perplexing was the fact the letter was typed and Mary Wallace only wrote her letters by hand. Also she did have a nephew with a brain ailment and had recently lectured to a club about her doll collection. She had not been in New York when the letter to Argentina was posted.

She held it for several days then decided to turn it over to postal authorities for whatever investigation they might deem it worth. To these authorities it seemed too pointless to be a joke. They turned it over to the FBI who likewise pondered the content and tried to make sense of it.

Often there is a dreamer, someone with a far ranging mind who will take such a project as having a definite purpose. There was one agent who had a theory.

He rationalized the "new dolls" were code names for warships operating in the Pacific. The term "Irish fisherman", he felt could mean an aircraft carrier since a carrier was draped in safety nets. The old woman with wood on her back could well stand for a warship with wooden superstructure and the little boy doll could stand for a new destroyer.

The dreamer stated the Mr. Shaw mentioned could well be the U.S.S. Shaw, badly damaged at Pearl Harbor. It had been repaired and was now operating in the Pacific. The postscript could well refer to the U.S.S. Louisville, a cruiser whose whereabouts was a closely guarded secret.

The postal authorities seemed amused by the interpretation but did not buy it.

Mary Wallace was questioned closely about her doll collection. She advised she had been to New York to add to her collection. She had talked with the owner and recalled mentioning the brain ailment of her nephew. She also admitted discussing her doll collection and ill nephew with others.

Committed to pursue the letter the agent went to other areas of contact such as art groups and hobby shops. He felt someone had a good knowledge of dolls, then went to see the doll shop in New York.

It was a high fashion shop that dealt in expensive and rare dolls. It was owned by Valvalee Dickinson who dealt in new and antique dolls. Prices began at fifty dollars. Velvalee turned out to be a small woman who did not look her fifty years. She weighed under 100 pounds

Agents lingered in her shop posing as potential customers but never revealing their true purpose. A background check of Mrs. Dickinson turned up nothing suspicious. She traveled often but it was in connection with her business—nothing suspicious.

Nevertheless the check continued including her outgoing mail. One day they discovered little notes tucked among the tissue paper of wrapped dolls. They were written in baby language but possibly contained some incriminating information.

During this time she was becoming nervous. Strange men were in her store constantly. From their questions it was obvious they knew little, if anything, about the dolls they supposedly wanted. Her mind worked overtime foreseeing her arrest. She considered flight and told her clerk she had to make a trip but would be back. She went to Portland to make contact with her Japanese superior. During the trip she made many desperate attempts to slip anyone who might be tailing her.

The FBI checked the hotels where she stayed and found three typewriters in various cities she had used. The type matched the Mary Wallace letter as did the misspelled words. When she reached Portland she found the restaurant where her Japanese contact was located, closed. She panicked. Having no place else to go she returned to her shop in New York rationalizing if the FBI was really on her tail she would have been arrested by now.

They were still definitely closing in but trying to alert contacts in South America to close the spy ring. Finally they struck. She had gone to her safe deposit box to recover a large amount of cash when they arrested her. It turned out the agent who originally surmised the Mary Wallace letter referred to naval ships was amazingly correct.

At her trial she confessed she was in need of money due to her age and the fact she had used all her money for her husband's health care. She received a ten-year sentence—but too late for Pearl Harbor.

XLI
Martha Dodd

This was a lady, the daughter of an American Ambassador, who spied for the Nazis. This same lady later became a spy for the Russians as World War II ended.

Her name was Martha Dodd. A spoiled daughter whose father was U.S. Ambassador to Germany, Dr. William E. Dodd, she grew up giving him constant problems. She was born in 1908 and grew up during Prohibition. One morning she came home to announce she had become married the night before. When asked her husbands name she didn't know. Her father found the name in the County Clerk's office and the marriage was quickly ended.

In college she became an avid reader, mostly of left wing material. A British professor, Robert M. Lovett, became her mentor and further inflamed her leftist leanings. In short order she quit college and took a job with the Chicago Tribune where she became even more enmeshed in communism, especially when she reviewed a book, Red Virtue, written by Ella Winter.

At the beginning of Hitler's rise in 1933 her father was appointed official U.S. Ambassador to Germany and went to Berlin. Martha, whose weakness was both sex and liquor, quickly shared both with many of the European men. Her language was extremely offensive when she was under the influence and embarrassed those around her.

When she arrived in Berlin she quickly fell in love with the Nazis. She was introduced to Hitler who had little interest in her. In one of her reports she talked of watching first hand the goose-stepping Nazis where she "heiled" as vigorously as any of them.

A woman on the move she soon ran across the concentration camps and saw the violence of the Nazis. Quickly she became disillusioned. Her Soviet contacts urged her to visit Russia which she did. She found it a paradise compared to Germany but she saw no evidences of brutality which were carefully concealed.

The Germans were taking all this in and in 1935 when she returned to Germany she was placed under surveillance. Even then she continued being invited to parties with high-ranking Nazis. She was invited to a party in the Russian Embassy celebrating their Nov. 7th revolution where she was greeted by Sergei M. Kudryavtsev. Ten years later he was to become head of their espionage operations in Canada.

Her brother Bill, became one of her fellow travelers. Bill was an intellectual with degrees from Chicago and Harvard. Martha had become involved with the International Peace Campaign and brought him in as a courier.

In 1937 Ambassador Dodd resigned his post and returned to the U.S along with Martha. She was introduced to President Roosevelt and became enchanted with him.

She met and married wealthy Alfred Stern. Together they threw parties that were so wild they outraged many of their neighbors. It took her less than two months to get him to switch from his formerly conservative ways to the communist cause.

When Pearl Harbor brought America into the war she became active as a Russian spy. She was cut out for the work and enlisted many of her friends. If idealism didn't work she was not above the use of blackmail. Her overseer was Anatol B. Gromov who was a secretary in the Soviet Embassy. She worked at stealing atomic secrets and at the end of the war became a courier to Mexico where the Soviet espionage headquarters were now located.

In 1953 the McCarthy anti-American Committee announced it was going to subpoena the daughter of a former U.S. Ambassador. Knowing it was her she and her husband liquidated everything they could and went to Mexico. From there, using forged passports they entered Switzerland and then went on to Prague. They moved into a large penthouse and immediately began throwing wild and lavish parties.

Nothing was heard of any espionage involvement thereafter.

XLII
Jane Anderson Aka "Lady Haw Haw"

As might be expected there are many propaganda ploys that backfire. The best laid plans of mice and men—goes a well known phrase by Robbie Burns.

Germany used a man known as Lord Haw-Haw to broadcast its tailored messages to England in particular. But less known was "Lady Haw-Haw" (so named by the British) who similarly told Germany's carefully tailored tales. She was a chubby American woman from Atlanta named Jane Anderson. In 1942 she began broadcasting over Germany's Zeesen transmitters. She was heard four times weekly as she aimed her drivel at her native country, America.

She had covered World War I for the London Daily Express and Daily Mail. She served as a correspondent in the Spanish Civil War. Many praised her as one of the great fighters against the Communist threat. Married to a Spanish Count, she was jailed in the early days of the Spanish civil war as an alleged spy working against Francisco Franco. It was the U.S. that intervened in her case, getting her released.

And now she suddenly appeared on Joseph Goebbel's radio. In March 1942 she made her big mistake. Attempting to 'set the record straight' about Germany's purported food shortages she broadcast about a recent visit to a German restaurant.

"On silver platters were sweets and cookies. 1 ate Turkish cookies, a delicacy I am very fond of. My friend ordered great goblets full of champagne into which he put shots of cognac to make it more lively. Sweets, cookies and champagne! Not bad!!"

"Big mistake", opined Allied experts.

The next night her text was translated into German and broadcast back to the German people who were standing in line for basic food supplies. The rebroadcast had its intended effect.

Jane Anderson aka Lady Haw-Haw was never heard from again.

Underground newspapers were extremely important to resistance forces. They encouraged donations and recruitment for their battered ranks. Because of German counter intelligence seeking these reporters and their presses it was often necessary to run their latest issue, then melt down the plates. They would then continue their normal business of printing for the Germans. A large Paris hotel was completely occupied by the Germans. An underground press existed in the basement. It was the same press that printed the daily menus. The Germans might have heard the presses rumbling but, knowing it printed the menus, paid it no heed.

An unnamed waitress who had just read the last underground paper noticed with horror a broken 't' letter that also appeared in the menu. How long would it be before a Gestapo agent noticed the same thing? The operation was quickly moved elsewhere.

XLIIII
Betty Pack Aka Cynthia Broussard

World War II brought a huge change in the use of women as agents. Due to sheer numbers of those involved in that war it would stand to reason there would be a likewise increase in women at risk. European countries did not display the same chivalrous (or maybe chauvinistic) code of protection for its women. England, France, Germany, Japan and Russia used women whereever they felt they could best serve. Gallant America, however, felt it best to continue protecting its women and used them sparingly. While the OSS had over 4,000 women in its organization only a few actually served in hazardous positions. Most were support where they performed admirably even though many yearned to get into the real action.

Red haired comedienne, Lucille Ball, became involved in one incident—not of her own making. She was returning from a visit to her dentist. On a lonely stretch of road her fillings began picking up the dit-dah of Morse code. She reported it to the FBI who traced down the sender in a gardener's tool shed. It was part of a Japanese espionage ring, quickly broken. It could be said some women were born with a single purpose—that of intrigue, espionage and seduction. Add to that intelligence and she becomes deadly. Such a woman was Betty Pack.

She was an American girl born in 1911. She was first recruited by the British as a spy in 1938, later served with the OSS. She freely admitted her greatest weapon was sex. She had an inborn knowledge of how to manipulate men and extract information from them over a hot pillow. She reported her bedroom work as 'expedient' and, when asked if she had any qualms about using her body, she replied, "Not in the least! My superiors told me that the results of my work saved thousands of British and American lives. Even one would have made it worthwhile.».wars are not won by 'respectable' methods.».».'

Her exploits extended far from the bedroom, however, and included burglary, safe cracking and assuming the false identity of a stepdaughter of a Vichy official. She spoke several languages fluently and was regarded as an accomplished journalist. Her other facets included her aloofness no doubt inspired by that of her highly educated mother, Cora Wells. Betty liked to spend much of her time alone in the woods listening to the wind rustling through the trees and sound of boats on

Maine's Casco Bay. She spoke of her ability to be comfortable in her own company.

In addition to her desire to be alone she had another passion—excitement. Any kind of excitement. She had a terrible restlessness and an 'excruciating sense of pressure' that was released only in action. She would run a race and when crossing the finish line continue on and on until her endurance expired. To her there was no sense in running unless she could run herself practically to death. It drove her brother, George, crazy.

In the upper strata of society she was presented to society in November 1929. At this time she met a British official, Arthur Pack. He was a large, impressive man who displayed a beautiful baritone voice. Betty was attracted to him in spite of the fact he was 20 years her senior.

They were thrown together a few days later at a house party. On the second night he retired to his room to find Betty, naked, lying in his bed.

Within a year she married him. It was just prior to her 19th birthday. From previous sexual encounters she was four months pregnant at the time but failed to inform her husband. The child was born abroad and put in the care of a foster couple. It was agreed papers would be adjusted later on to give the child a proper date that coincided with his parents marriage.

Arthur was first assigned to South America where Betty soon bedded several influential men. In March 1934 her husband was posted to the British Embassy in Madrid. Betty was in love with Spain and spoke Spanish fluently. In short order she found new lovers.

Spain gave her her very first taste of actual action. In 1935, during the Spanish war, she was arrested as a spy but later released. She returned and in doing so figured a plan to smuggle five loyalists out of enemy territory posing them as drunks jammed into the back of her car. After passing numerous sentries and conning them they were let out in neutral territory. The adrenalin high and post climactic rush she experienced were as great as any sex act. She was hooked.

In a bold move to find a Spanish lover who had disappeared she went to see the Minister of Defense, one Prieto. She managed not only to gain her lover's release but also 17 airmen who faced possible execution as enemies of the loyalist forces.

In late 1937 her husband was posted to Warsaw and on the last day of that year suffered a severe disabling stroke. He was sent back to London for treatment while Betty remained and found a Polish friend, Edward Kulikowsky, who lived in an apartment across from her own.

Before long they were sipping vodka in his apartment where he played the piano. They made love on a bear rug in front of his fireplace. One day Kulikowsky casually mentioned that Hitler was going to invade Czechoslovakia and soon after that, Poland. She gave the information to a British S1S (Secret Intelligence Service) agent who relayed it to higher authorities. Adding this bit of intelligence to the job she had done in Spain led the SIS to realize her potential and officially put her to work in March of 1938.

As the war drums increased their ominous beating it soon was apparent to the British their only reliable agent in all of Poland was Betty. She bedded Michal Lubienski who ran the Foreign Minister's office and therefore had access to all the secret papers his office encountered.

There was a division within England regarding the intelligence produced by Betty. Neville Chamberlain turned up his nose at the matter in which the material was procured. It did not fit the proper British standards. On the other hand Winston Churchill had no compunctions saying he would accept anything that would help defeat Hitler.

Through her paramour contacts Betty stumbled into one of the most closely guarded secrets of WWII. It was the Enigma encoding machine. The Germans adapted it for their military and began manufacturing them by the thousands. A complicated machine it was felt that it could never be broken. The British felt the Poles had somehow solved it but needed some verification. Betty was able to supply information on the Polish crypt-analysis unit in the Kabacki Woods just south of Warsaw in the town of Pyry.

A noted author on the subject of espionage, Richard Deacon, had an interview with those involved with the early days of Enigma. They reported Betty had Michal bring sensitive documents on the machine to her which she photographed and sent on to SIS. They reported it as an incredible find providing the missing link and putting it into layman terms so we could understand it much easier.

The subject was so secret little was ever said. One reference came from William Stevenson, biographer of Sir William Stephenson, (a man called Intrepid) who said, "In 1971 or 1972 (I will have to check) General Sir Colin

Gubins spoke of Betty in 1938 in connection with Enigma after receiving a cable from Sir William to talk freely to me...." Intelligence sent to London was classified by MI6 under one of the following categories:

A. Very reliable (inside source)
B. Fairly reliable
C. Uncertain reliability
D. Doubtful reliability
1. At first-hand
2. At second-hand
3. At second-hand uncertain
4. Rumour

They had little choice but to classify Betty's information from Lubienski as Al. At the same time, however, her contact with the Pole was causing much concern within the diplomatic corps, especially the wives.

As the war drew nearer Betty was asked to leave Warsaw. Not wanting to separate from Lubienski she protested but to no avail. In essence she was thrown out of Poland by the British who felt she was becoming a liability. Also when the Germans invaded and realized what she had been about her life would be threatened.

Sadly she returned to France where she learned her husband had been greatly improved through therapy. He was being posted to Chile. Betty found sadness in the fact she was out of touch with British intelligence which was a major part of her life. She became alarmed over the Chilean affinity for the Germans and put her thoughts down which she gave to the British Ambassador.

Alarmed at the Pro-German articles appearing in a local paper she made arrangements to write her own stories in another paper that were critical of Germany. She produced a copy of a map she had stolen in Poland showing German plans to take Yugoslavia, Bulgaria and Rumania in 1940 followed by France, Belgium, Switzerland, Luxemburg, Holland, Belgium and Denmark in 1941 and then Russia. The German Ambassador took a dim view of her articles and protested the wife of a British diplomat writing such "lies". She was in her glory—in the midst of another battle.

But now other plans were being made by Betty. They did not include her husband or child. She had been in contact with SIS and, aware of her potential to gather intelligence, told her (in typically British understatement) that should she return to England she might be of assistance in the war effort. That was all she needed. Leaving Chile she told Arthur it was for a brief visit with her mother. In her heart she had no thought of returning but rather of going into Europe as an agent. Their child, Denise, now age 5, was left in the care of Juanquita, her nanny. While Betty never had any close friends among the Embassy wives due to her lifestyle, the abandoning of her child to a nanny was the final straw. They all strongly condemned her.

By the middle of 1940 Germany had driven all the way to the English Channel. England had established various military groups for its women. But there was a new, shadowy group, the SOE (Special Operations Executive) that offered a highly dangerous opportunity in intelligence and covert operations.

A debate explored whether or not women could be properly used in such operations. Winston Churchill resolved it by saying that in a fight with the Nazis no holds out to be barred. The SOE became official July 22, 1940. Women were to be used and treated as equals.

Travel was tight and required special permits. She was able to wind up in New York after circuitous flights from Chile. The British picked her up and she soon was working for the BSC (British Security Coordination). Her target was at first the Italian codes. She had a torrid affair with Italian Admiral Albarto Lais and soon procured their codes as well as a major plan of sabotage.

America had not yet entered the war but anticipating its entry Italy had ordered its ships at various ports be sabotaged. The Admiral told her he had already given orders for five ships in the Norfolk shipyard to be blown up and the charges were set. In addition one was to be sunk in the Panama canal.

As America was neutral its military could not act. It took an order from President Roosevelt to authorize the Coast Guard to board and save the ships. Many had already been severely damaged by the time the blue jacketed Coast Guardsmen arrived.

The Italian codes were of great use to the British and later the Americans when the invasion of North Africa began. The entry into war after Pearl Harbor changed the rules of the game—if there ever were any.

The Germans rapidly overran Poland and France. A portion of south France was allowed to remain free under the French Vichy government whose loyalty was extremely questionable.

Her next objective became the Vichy French. She actually became involved in the safe cracking to obtain the codebooks which were returned to her apartment, photographed, then returned. The operation involved three break-ins, use of a safe cracker from prison and the drugging of a night watchman and his dog. Following that she prepared to go into France as the stepdaughter of a French official, Charles Brousse, with whom she quickly became sexually involved.

With relations broken between the Vichy Government and America it became impossible for Betty and her 'step-father' to return in that capacity. In late 1942 she came under control of the OSS. Delay followed delay in getting her out of America and into France. In the end she was destined to spend the final days of the war in America. But destiny had intervened for the Germans were all too well aware of this woman and were waiting for her to appear.

At wars end she moved to a small town in France where her now legal husband, Charles Brousse, had holdings. She died of cancer Dec. 1, 1963.

Controversy continued swirling around the lady as stories began appearing in London periodicals immediately prior to her death. Records do substantiate the fact she had been instrumental in stealing both the French and Italian codes and was involved in the Enigma project. A high placed OSS official commented the stolen codebooks had been of great value in the North Africa operations.

CHAPTER 6

---▼---

XLIV
Agnes Smedley

In the 1930s Agnes Smedley was an American writer with decidedly leftist leanings. She had a big following in liberal circles. Gradually she drifted into Communism where she became not only a fellow traveler but actually a spy.

She worked for not only Russia but China. Soviet spy-master, Richard Sorge, was allowed use of her apartment as a base. In addition Agnes helped recruit Ozaki Hozumi, also a writer for her Japanese countrymen. Hozumi was a dedicated leftist. She became a main link between Soviet and Chinese communists.

A major break through came at the outset of WWII. President Roosevelt appointed Smedley as one of the advisers to General Joseph Stilwell who was the adviser to Generalissimo Chiang Kai-shek. As was to be expected by Stilwell she used all her efforts to get the bulk of military supplies sent north to the forces of Mao Tse-tung.

Stilwell, even knowing what she was, did cooperate because he felt Mao was efficiently fighting the Japanese while Chiang Kai-shek was burying all equipment and waiting for the eventual show down with Mao's forces.

Soviet spymaster, Sorge, a complete chauvinist, said of her, "She was a woman with a brilliant mind»..»she was like a man."

The Commander of the Chinese Communists was Chu-teh and he became a close friend of hers. He later fought against America in Korea.

As the war ended she was driven out of China by the American China Lobby. In death she gave her ashes and all property to Chu-teh. Her ashes were interred in Peking.

1^

XLV
Sylvia Ageloff

This is the case of a woman being duped—becoming a conduit that brought about the assassination of one of the worlds best known men.

The setting was Vienna, the time 1938. Sylvia Ageloff was a 27 year old psychologist employed by the New York City Board of Education. She was somewhat adventuresome and felt drawn to the cradle of psychology in Vienna. Her guru, Dr. Freud, was in London and she had hopes of seeing him as she traveled around Europe.

After taking in a few of the local sites she sat down in a coffee shop and there met Jacques Monard, a most attractive man. He told her he was a journalism student at the Sorbonne. He appeared well educated and well heeled. He took her around Paris to the finest restaurants and nightspots. He said he was from an old Belgian family.

Sylvia, seeking to impress him with her side of the family said she had recently visited her sister in Mexico City. Then added her sister is a Trotskyite and worked for Leon Trotsky.

It went over his head. He advised he had no interest in politics, only in becoming a famous author. He further added he considered politics dirty and wanted no part of them.

Sylvia soon ran out of money and advised him she would have to return to America. He wanted her to stay and found a temporary job for her. But he found it necessary to return to his home in Belgium for a few days. His mother had been seriously injured in a car accident. In February 1939 he wrote to tell her he had been appointed as a foreign correspondent to the United States and she should return home. He would follow.

She got a job with the Brooklyn Welfare Department. Jacues arrived in September 1939, just as WWII broke out. He had a new name—Frank Jacson. The reason he gave was that as a Belgian citizen he was eligible for the draft and would never have been given permission to emigrate. He did it out of his deep love for her, he said.

The next month he went to Mexico City. For several weeks he wrote love letters saying how much he missed her and appealing for her to join him. His new job provided plenty of money. Two months later Sylvia took a leave of absence and joined him in Mexico City. She was deliriously happy. Her sister still worked for Leon Trotsky and was introduced to the now Frank Jacson.

In March 1940 Sylvia had to return to her job. Frank stayed behind with the new friends he had met through Sylvia's sister. He was especially close to the Rosmers who had been France's Communist leaders. They were expelled by the Comintern due to their close ties to Trotsky.

On May 24, 1940, an attempt was made on Trotsky's life. His residence, even his bedroom was sprayed with automatic rifle fire. Trotsky and his wife had hidden under the bed when the firing started and were spared.

Frank Jacson was there the next day and did some kind things for them. He met Trotsky face to face for the first time. After that he became a welcome fixture in the Trotsky household.

In August Sylvia took her vacation and visited them in Mexico City. The Trotsky's had them all to tea. In a political discussion Jacson exhibited an interest in politics for the first time. He sided with Trotsky against Sylvia.

A week after that date Jacson returned to the home and said he had written an article he wanted Trotsky to read. The two went into the house.

A few minutes later Mrs. Trotsky reported hearing "a terrible, soul-shaking cry-prolonged and agonized half scream, half sob." Rushing into the room she saw her husband down with an ice pick plunged into his brain. He died twenty-six hours later.

As Jacson was arrested he was quick to proclaim, "They made me do it. They have imprisoned my mother. Sylvia had nothing to do with it".

Sylvia was outraged. She called him a dirty Russian OGPU agent and murderer. She added she never wanted to see him again.

Today he lives in relative comfort in a Mexican prison. Plenty of money is available to him through his attorney. And so Persian-born Jacques Mornard Vandendreschd, one of history's best-known assassins, spends his final days.

XLVI
Therese Bonney

Prior to the war between Finland and Russia, a free lance American correspondent, Therese Bonney, had interviewed Finland's Marshal Mannerheim. She did so for the Colliers magazine. He had been the hero of a brave resistance put up by the Finns against the over-whelming numerical superiority of Russian forces. As the war progressed and Germany occupied Finland OSS contacted Bonney to visit Helsinki and get an interview with Mannerheim. It was understood special notes and instructions would go with her.

She arrived in Helsinki but found her way blocked by the Gestapo. Through subterfuge and help of the under-ground she nevertheless did manage to see him. Nothing was accomplished and it was never known just what information she brought back.

Before returning home she stopped off in Sweden to visit an old friend in the Foreign Service. Without revealing her affiliation she asked him what he thought of OSS.

He replied, "We can always smell an OSS person. We never give 'em any help".

XLVII
Virginia Hall

One of OSS' most outstanding women operators in France was British trained Virginia Hall, the only American civilian woman to receive the Distinguished Service Cross for heroism. She was also awarded the British MBE.

She was born in Baltimore in 1906. Early on she sought adventure. She did not fit into the rigid academic life at Radcliff and Barnard and persuaded her family to let her go to Europe where she finished her studies in Paris and Vienna. She returned home for graduate study at George Washington University in Washington.

Employed by the Foreign Service department she was sent to Turkey. There, in a hunting accident, she lost part of one leg below the knee. She learned to use her artificial limb with only a slight limp. When the war broke out she went to Paris to enlist as an ambulance driver. Speaking French, German and Italian she was a natural and soon joined Britain's SOE. When France was overrun she crossed the Pyrenees on foot. SOE assigned her to Madrid but it was not enough. She wanted to be in on D-Day.

From there she petitioned OSS and was accepted. She went back into France and worked as a milkmaid, taking cows to pasture, cooking meals for her farmer hosts and doing the wash in rocky streams. Alternately she carried out her real mission: sending and receiving radio traffic and organizing parachute drops.

The Germans were on the outlook for her and checked carefully for this woman they called the 'limping lady' due to her artificial foot. It was necessary to disguise her slender figure with bulky clothing and dye her hair a dirty grey.

She referred to her artificial limb as 'Cuthbert' and worked through her pain. In one message to Headquarters in London she said Cuthbert "was giving her a bad time."

An officer on the other end, not knowing who or what Cuthbert was, sent back a message saying

"If he is giving you trouble, eliminate him." Although she had no training in sabotage, for six months in the wake of the Allied advance her teams had blown four bridges, destroyed a key rail line in several places, cut telephone wires and derailed freight trains.

She was so modest that when awarded the Distinguished Service Cross at wars end she refused to accept it publicly and did so only in General Donovan's office. After the war she was one of the first woman officers employed by the Central Intelligence Agency.

XLIIII
Claire Phillips Aka High Pockets

One of the strongest motives for becoming a spy is love of country. Another is to seek revenge. Both were responsible for Claire Phillips, an average American housewife.

It began with World War II and the Japanese capture of Corregidor. Her husband was captured and later killed by the Japanese forces. She knew she must avenge his death.

Because she had lived in Manila prior to the war the Japanese did not intern her as they did with most Caucasians. Giving it her all Claire sold her jewels and all other possessions and opened a nightclub on the Manila waterfront. By chance it happened to provide a clear view of Japanese naval activity in the harbor.

And now playing the game to the hilt she plied the Japanese officers with liquor and flattered them. In turn they gave out some information that later proved vital to the Allied war effort. An American army Captain with guerrilla forces in the hills gave her the code name of HIGH POCKETS. Through a series of sentries she was able to relay information to him.

She was the first to provide the information Japanese were using Red Cross ships to transport troops. But her biggest coup was giving the exact time Japanese carriers were leaving for the Solomon Islands where they suffered a major defeat.

XLIX
American Ex-Patriate #1

To add to these stories there are at least two more that are a welcome relief. One concerns an elderly American lady who remained in France after it fell. She wanted to be with her daughter who happened to be married to a French underground leader. In her own right the older lady was an important figure in Allied secret services.

Near the end of 1941 her apartment was occupied by two German officers over whom she had no control. She worked extremely carefully knowing they had access to every nook and cranny of the small apartment they all occupied. She never spoke to them unless she had to. They remained equally aloof—always proper but never exchanging small talk.

One day they told her they must leave. She replied coldly, the sooner the better as far as she was concerned. They stood stiffly at attention holding a small wrapped box. With heels clicking and a stiff bow they handed it to her.

"Please accept this as a token of our gratitude—but we ask you not open it for twenty-four hours", they instructed.

The woman and her maid gladly watched them depart but did honor their request in delaying the opening of the box. When they did they found a silver cigarette box. Inside was a note that said, "With many thanks from two members of the British Secret Service."

L
American Ex-Patriate #2

The second story is a favorite of OSS Commandant, General William Donovan. It likewise revolves around an elderly American lady who had married a French Count and was widowed. She had an apartment in Paris and a villa in the countryside. Knowing she had no reason to fear the Germans she remained behind. The Germans felt the kindly old lady was harmless and gave her a pass allowing her to travel freely between her two residences.

It didn't take long for OSS to realize this lady would be a wonderful courier and she agreed to carry messages for them. One extremely hot day she was traveling by train from her villa into Paris. She had need to visit the lavatory. Knowing of the severe paper shortage and that there would be no toilet seat covers she took a page from her newspaper, tore it to fit and spread it over the toilet seat. Her hot and perspiring skin picked up the print, transferring it to her derriere.

As she left the lavatory the train stopped. The Germans were pulling a surprise inspection. The passengers were taken into the station. The men in one room, the ladies in another. All were ordered to strip. The Countess protested this indignity but the stout German matron insisted there would be no exceptions.

As the matron encircled the now nude women she came across the printed buttocks and exclaimed, "Aha".

Feeling she had caught a fish she made the Countess bend over while she scanned the print. She called for a mirror and transferred the French words onto a pad. Not knowing French she marched proudly to her commander and handed him the 'incriminating' evidence on the 'spy'.

A few minutes later she returned and icily told the women to get dressed and get back on the train. Her commander had obviously translated some of the French newspaper for her.

In the uproar of the event they failed to check her purse which contained seven OSS messages in the lining.

LI
Ruth Kuehn

The minister for propaganda in the Nazi party was Dr. Joseph Goebbels. His strong sexual drive was centered especially on young girls.

At a high level party he met Ruth Kuehn. Her father was Bernard Julius Otto Kuehn who claimed a close friendship with Gestapo chief Heinrich Himmler. It didn't take long for Goebbels to add the seventeen year-old beauty to his stable of mistresses.

Shortly after that his ardor cooled and because of that, and some pressure from his other mistresses, he decided it was time for her to go. He found the perfect out when Japan told him they sought some Europeans to spy for them. Ruth and her father were ordered to Hawaii and departed for Honolulu in 1939.

Dr. Kuehn's cover was that of a linguist and an interest in Hawaii. It enabled him to travel freely. He was gone for long periods of time gathering his information and relaying items of interest to the Japanese. Ruth often accompanied him while his wife, Friedel, stayed home playing the dutiful housewife role.

Ruth grew more beautiful and was in constant demand for parties that included many military officers. She both charmed and bedded them extracting considerable information. In addition she worked the wives by opening a beauty parlor where gossip flowed freely along with news of the Pacific fleet.

During the 1936–1941 period Ruth made two trips to Japan in the role of a courier. Neither the FBI or Navy Intelligence paid it much heed. While Germany had loaned them to Japan they suddenly decided they had a stake in their operation. General Haushofer, who had sent them, demanded all of their report come through him first. Because they were now working for two governments the Kuehns decided they were worth more and asked for it. Ruth was living the high life to the fullest.

Her father said he had need of a more quiet place for his work and in 1939 moved the family to Pearl Harbor. The seeds were already growing.

Japanese Vice-Counsel Otojiro Okuda invited Ruth and her father to join him one day. It was time, he informed them, for some detailed information such as dates, locations and figures on American Naval forces. He said their past work was good but this new information was vital and they would be well paid. Ruth asked for $40,000. It was negotiated down to a $14,000 advance with the balance to be paid upon delivery.

Her father was concerned over how they would get the information. It was a simple matter to Ruth. She became engaged to one of the highest-ranking Naval officers stationed at Pearl Harbor. Together with her fiance they strolled daily among the fortified sections of Pearl Harbor. She insisted her ten-year old brother accompany them as he was just wild about the U.S. Navy and its ships. The American soldiers took to the boy and invited him aboard a battleship explaining armaments and other items. He retained as much as possible and was debriefed by Ruth and her father.

Now really into the game, Ruth figured out a way to transmit information on the kinds and numbers of ships at anchor. The Kuehn's owned a second home at Kalama not far from the harbor. She bought a pair of high power binoculars and worked out a light signal procedure. It was perfected between the Kuehns, Okuda and the fourth secretary of the Japanese Consulate, Tadesi Morimura. On December 2, 1941, they gave it the first trial run. It worked to perfection•

They laid out a blueprint of Pearl Harbor. From the bits and pieces of information they assembled the layout of ships at anchor, the arrival, departure and destination of U.S. warships. On the morning of December 7, 1941 they threw open the window of their Kalama home and gave the first deadly light signals. Directing the enemy bombers to the best targets they also told them what not to bomb. On that dark morning the two directed the Pearl Harbor attack.

All seemed going well for them but soon things began to unravel. The Japanese had arranged for them to be picked up by a submarine that would take them to Tokyo. The Kuehn's would take only the cash on hand and collect the balance on their arrival. Two U.S. Intelligence officers, however, had spotted the lights flashing from the Kuehn residence and went to investigate. They found a blueprint of the signal system, the powerful binoculars and a large amount of cash, some Japanese. Her father tried to shield his family and said he was totally responsible for the whole operation. Ruth likewise said she was in charge.

On February 21, 1942, Dr. Kuehn was sentenced to be shot. Ruth's trial was coming up and he was greatly concerned. He tried to make a deal but was told the American government didn't make deals with Nazis. But finally there was clemency after he agreed to tell the entire story of German and Japanese espionage. He was sentenced to thirty years hard labor at Alcatraz.

Ruth and her mother were interned and later returned to Germany. Ruth has a sister living in Los Angeles under a different name. She gave the information for this story.

LII
Baroness Anna Wolkoff

Anna Wolkoff had been a British citizen from early childhood. She nevertheless used the title of Baroness which had been conferred on her father by the Czar. He had been an admiral in the Imperial Fleet. After the Russian Revolution he took his family and fled to London.

Anna was a strong woman with a flair for the dramatic. She ran an exclusive dress shop in London hiring only attractive, well-shaped salesladies. She always wore a gorgeous ginger cat pin wearing a gold collar.

Among her other outlets was painting. She dabbled in paintings and occasionally had showings in local galleries. Whether it was at one of these exhibitions or elsewhere is not known but she did meet a young American diplomat. He was twenty-four while she was thirty seven. In spite of her thirteen-year seniority they hit it off but not for the same reasons. He was Tyler Kent, an all American name to be sure. He had attended Princeton, then the Sorbonne in Paris, the University of Madrid and the George Washington University in Washington, D.C. Kent was the son of a Foreign Service officer and followed his father's footsteps by entering government service when he was twenty one. He first served in Moscow. In 1939 he was sent to the Embassy in London where he continued his job as a code clerk. During his brief service he had picked up other languages and could speak Russian, French, German and Italian.

War had not yet begun in 1939 but was obviously on the immediate horizon. Talk was centered on the subject. Tyler hated war and immediately sympathized with those groups who opposed it. He was taken in by the Nazis talk of peace.

He was drawn deeper and deeper into the well sounding propaganda of the Fascists who only preached peace. He totally bought the proclamations of the Anglo-German Fellowship which contained many Britons. In particular he became convinced of a Jewish conspiracy and that they were responsible for the war which had now begun.

The Baroness feeling that the timing was right began to prevail on him She suggested the war could be ended soon and long lasting friendship would endure between the Germans and Allies if only Tyler could reveal some of those sinister conspiracies perpetrated by Jewish interests.

She knew he saw the most highly secret messages between Churchill and Roosevelt. Indeed every message between Neville Chamberlain and President Roosevelt had gone through his room. What about those messages carried by couriers showing extremely sensitive problems with armament and American supplies. All Tyler had to do was find the most sensitive ones and get them to the Baroness. She would see they would find their way to proper authorities in the Axis side and further the aims of a lasting peace.

The matter was handled simply. At night Tyler would take the incriminating documents home with him. The Baroness would photo them and they would be returned the next morning.

While this was going on Scotland Yard became interested in Tyler. By infiltrating Fascist groups they had discovered him and heard him proclaiming the anti-Jewish line and expressing pro-German sentiments.

Because Tyler held diplomatic immunity they went to U.S. Ambassador, Joseph Kennedy, to ask for a waiver of such immunity. They wanted to search Tyler's apartment. He agreed.

Early one morning after he had left for work they went into the apartment to begin their search. It didn't take long to find extremely incriminating documents. He had over 1,500 papers as well as some duplicate keys to the code room. He had these made in case he was transferred to another department.

The net had been tightening around the Baroness. British Secret Service kept a close watch on foreign born, especially if they were involved with diplomatic officials and attended pro-Fascist meetings.

In tailing the Baroness first, then together with Tyler, they found after meeting in her apartment they would go out. Not for dinner or the theatre but to a photo studio. Under the guise of a security lecture a British detective visited the photo studio. Then he brought up the subject of the foreign lady and her male companion.

The photographer said there was nothing to worry about there. The lady was a diplomatic official and he was simply doing work for the U.S. Embassy. He had no qualms about showing a sample of his work by exhibiting negatives of work then in process. The papers were almost all marked 'Top Secret'. Convinced he had been duped and thought he was honestly doing work for the U.S. Embassy, they did not charge him.

A hurriedly called conference was held at 10 Downing Street. It contained all top-level British officials plus Ambassador Kennedy. The Ambassador was stunned at the betrayal. He sat in on the meeting with British officials as they charged Tyler with espionage.

So severe was the damage that all American diplomatic communications were discontinued for a period of six to eight weeks. This was at the height of the fall of France and the Dunkirk disaster. Special couriers were sent world wide to distribute new codes.

For a period of eight months it was obvious the Germans and Japanese knew everything that had gone in and out of the State Department.

During his trial Kent was never remorseful and took occasion to continue haranging 'Jewish lackies' responsible for the war. His only concern was the welfare of the Countess.

He was sentenced to seven years in prison on November 7, 1940. The Countess received a ten-year sentence but was released after serving five and a half years. She had well served the Fascist cause.

LIII
Adrienne

She was called by many the cleverest spy in the Balkans during World War II.

It was in April 1940 she danced her way into the hearts of patrons at the Budapest cabaret, 'Papagallo'. Here she met the new Ambassador to Bulgaria, George Howard Earle, who later became the Governor of Pennsylvania.

She was quick-witted, intelligent and spoke many languages. She was comfortable in the highest circles. Her
aunt was Madame Lupescu, later the wife of Rumanian
ex-King Carol. Her father was well known and brought
her up in a highly sophisticated society. Ambassador
Earle quickly realized he had a top notch spy in
Adrienne. He put her up in a hotel in Sofia and thereafter got a house for her near a park. An alleged Albanian
journalist called Diello called on her occasionally. She
made trips several times to Lake Ochrida for vacations
and there was also seen in the company of Diello.

In late 1942 the Bulgarian government for unknown
reasons said they would not be unhappy should our government decide to send a different Ambassador. In
January 1943 Earle was sent to Istanbul as Naval Attache.

He tried to bring Adrienne with him feeling her
invaluable. But she was thwarted at the border and had
to return to her nightclub. One night, her act finished,
she was visited by a strange man in her dressing room.
He said he brought her greetings from an Albanian
named Diello who was now in Ankara.

The stranger was one of Kaltenbrunner's agents in
Budapest. Kaltenbrunner, who headed German intelligence in the area, had employed Diello who in turn had
hired Adrienne to ferret secrets from Earle. Adrienne
was anxious to get to Ankara for she had fallen for
Diello and in addition wanted to keep tabs on Earle's
activities. The Germans definitely wanted her with
Earle and put pressure on the Turkish government to
admit her. It worked.

In her first meeting with her Albanian lover he told
her he was working as a valet to the Chief Councillor of

the German Embassy at Ankara. She found it hard to comprehend German intelligence would be spying on its own people. The fact various factions of the German government were spying on each other for political gain was beyond her.

And then an amazing stroke of good luck hit Diello. He got a job as valet to British Ambassador Sir Hughe Knatchbull-Hugessen. Expecting the information to flow, the Germans were disappointed. The British Ambassador was highly security minded and left nothing lying around. Days went by until one memorable day when Diello reported there was to be a meeting of the Big Three, Roosevelt, Churchill and Stalin. Location not yet known.

Hitler and his aides were ecstatic. Diello, striking while the iron was hot, asked for $30,000 in U.S. currency. The Germans watched the papers carefully for days for confirmation of the story.

Nothing came. They wanted to talk with Diello and dispatched a group of their top agents to Ankara. Since they could not be seen with Diello they worked through Adrienne. Through her they said the money would be forthcoming provided first there be reports in the press confirming the meeting and, second, could he prove he could keep them informed of the progress of the meeting. Diello blew their minds when he told them he had stolen the key to the safe and had it duplicated. He could read everything nightly, make copies and return any documents without detection.

And then the confirmation of the Big Three meeting came from the press. The Germans were beside themselves with glee. They paid the $30,000 to Diello and more. Adrienne remained the intermediary between Kaltenbrunner and Diello and was equally well rewarded financially. Without her there would have been extreme problems in connecting the Germans and Diello.

They named it 'Operation Cicero'.

Diello informed them there was dissension between the three world leaders. Churchill violently opposed a French invasion. He opted for the Mediterranean with landings in the Dodecanese Islands and Greece. His reasoning was that unless they operated within the Balkans the Russians would eventually take over militarily and politically .

The Germans were delighted, sensing a deep disagreement between these uneasy Allies. Diello played them masterfully by being silent for a while and upping his ante, then showering them with more startling information. Adrienne was able to add her own interpretations to the Germans as she hand delivered documents and answered their personal questions.

Stalin, he reported, had bluntly informed Roosevelt and Churchill that it was still possible for the Soviets to come to an agreement with the Third Reich. This they would prefer to loss of the Balkans through an invasion of American-British forces. He demanded an invasion through France which Roosevelt also supported against Churchill. Finally Diello advised he had the full details of all meetings and would deliver them for $100,000 American currency which was agreed to.

The plane arriving delivered the funds and the full Teheran report was given over. The question today is whether the report was slanted to confuse the Germans and convince them Churchill would overrule the French landing and come through middle Europe. Some analysts today feel the Germans were so convinced of that possibility they left lighter forces at Normandy pending a possible Balkan assault.

The big winners were Diello and Adrienne who disappeared into South America with nearly $250,000 although there exists the possibility many of the American dollars were counterfeit. They did turn up in America seeking an audience with Earle but what transpired then and where they wound up is not known.

LIV
Vera De Witte Aka Vera Erikson

An important link in Hitler's plan to control the world was the subjugation of England. His operation, LENA, was designed to begin operations preparatory to actual invasion of the island. Agents of LENA were to select those beach sites and air-drop sites to receive German troops.

Three agents were involved: Major Hans Dierks, Theo Druecke and a beautiful Nordic blonde, codename Vera Erikson. She also was the mistress of Dierks.

Vera was actually Vera de Witte, daughter of a Russian naval officer who died fighting the Bolsheviks. After his death his wife escaped to Copenhagen taking Vera and her brother. Vera met and married a Frenchman and moved to Paris where he abandoned her. She was reduced to living with different men and dancing wherever she could. One of her lovers was a dancer who actually served the Russian secret police. He soon convinced Vera she should also work for the GPU. He soon turned sour. One night in a back alley he turned on Vera and tried to stab her. Fortunately Druecke, who was touring night spots, came upon them and saved her.

He took her to Brussels and introduced her to Dierks who quickly seduced her and made her his mistress. Dierks happened to be an Abwehr (German) agent. He realized she had a special talent of obtaining information from men and moved her to England. There she was put in the home of a British naval air officer. She also met May Erikson who also was providing information to the Germans. Her code name was Lady May.

Through various contacts Vera was offered a position in a tea room sponsored by the Duchess Chateau-Thierry, a widow, also an Abwehr agent. The plan was for Vera to seduce British officers and politicians and gather intelligence for Germany.

It was aborted when Dierks returned to Hamburg and insisted she join him. It was at this time LENA was organized and Dierks ordered to England.

Prior to his departure a final farewell dinner was held with Dierks, Druecke and Vera. With too many drinks the inevitable auto accident occurred where Dierks was killed.

LENA was reorganized with Druecke and Vera who were to leave Sept. 30, 1938. On that date a seaplane deposited them off the Banffshire coast. They stepped into their rubber dinghy, together with the bicycles they would need, and headed for the shore. They were swamped and arrived ashore dripping wet. Their bicycles were lost.

In trying to get themselves oriented they went to a railway station where a clerk, suspicious of their wet clothing and questions, called the police. Incriminating guns and explosives told the police all they needed to know.

Druecke was found guilty and hanged. Vera was able to throw enough smoke using the name of Lady May and the British home she had once occupied to get her off.

In some manner she was released and returned to Germany where she worked for the Abwehr during WWII.

CHAPTER 7

▼

British Women

The British were quick to use their women even for the most dangerous operations. At Arising, Scotland they went through final training which included silent killing and use of weapons of both sides. They were briefed in security measures including how to conceal their radio sets. They were also given pills: cyanide pills to take in case of capture; pills to keep them awake; pills to put in drinks that would knock out their enemy; even pills that would produce intestinal symptoms if they needed to feign illness. An efficient, motherly woman, Vera Atkins gave them last minute information on rationing, work and travel regulations. She checked their clothes to be certain they were cut in the European style, usually by a trusted and cleared Polish refugee tailor in London. Even the items in their pockets were carefully planted. Cigarette tobacco had to match that being used in France. Theater stubs must jibe with the area in which the agent was operating. Spare pocket change must ring true. If the woman was a heavy smoker her nicotine stains in tobacco-short

Europe would give her away. They had to be removed with a pumice stone. They were slipped into Europe via boat and parachute. They worked under the SOE auspices. Their code designations were registered in a modest house at 64 Baker Street, London with typical British understatement.

LV
Dorothy Pamela O'grady

She appeared as from the mists. One day she was...just there. No one knew where she came from but she was living with her husband on the Isle of Wight in the days prior to World War II. Her husband was retired on a modest pension. They kept to themselves and were considered part of the normal, quiet scene in that area.

There was no discussion of the boarders she took in to augment their income. German tourists were not uncommon in those days and they kept to themselves. The locals were not disturbed.

Mrs. O'Grady took to sketching, a not uncommon hobby. She would go up into the hills and sketch the seacoast or clouds or the birds that flew overhead.

Mr. O'Grady took no interest in her sketches. He never asked to see what she was doing. Even when she spent time near the huge towers the British were constructing on the coast.

When war broke out he volunteered to be a fireman and left for England. She remained behind in their home at Sandown.

But she was not alone. Scotland Yard had taken an interest in those coming and going from the small island. While being tailed she led them to some interesting contacts known to be German. Her home was searched and revealed a treasure trove of documents and sketches that related to the Canadian First Division which was stationed nearby.

The Isle of Wight was to be a jumping off point for eleven Nazi divisions destined to invade England. Her sketches of the harbors and other facilities were hidden in furniture and behind pictures that hung on the wall.

Her trial was held in Great Hall of Winchester Castle on December 17, 1940. She was eloquent in her defense and denied her work was designed to aid the enemy. Even the prosecutor had to admire her as she faced them single handed.

She did not win the jury, however. She was found guilty. Her sentence was fourteen years.

When she was released she faced a world far different from what she had envisioned and worked for.

LVI
Adrienne #2

The OSS hired many nationals for its work in Europe. Who better qualified to penetrate Holland than a person who was born and raised there—or any of the European countries.

One woman, a Belgian, was known only as Adrienne in the records. She made her initial jump into Belgium and was never heard from. It was assumed she died then or later at the hands of the Germans.

As the war pushed deep into Germany in the final days. Gen. Donovan visited the infamous Dachau concentration camp. It was there he found Adrienne, near death. The once vibrant, attractive woman with laughing eyes and flashing white teeth had been subjected to horrible torture.

The sadistic guards had removed all her teeth and shaved her head. Her face sagged grotesquely over her gums and her blue yes stared blankly from sunken sockets. Donovan held back tears as he bent over her fragile, tragic figure.

He immediately arranged for her to be flown to the best hospital available in England where she was treated. When they had done all for her that they could they returned her to her native Belgium.

The horror of the experience, however, was too great. A year after the war ended she was found hanging from a rod in her clothes closet.

These Also Served

Most of the non-professional woman agents served briefly and bravely before returning to their regular lifestyle. It is sad they will never really be recognized for their bravery and ingenuity which saved many Allied lives.

Women, boys and girls volunteered to penetrate enemy lines to secure intelligence information. Women were found to be especially useful for this short range work because they attracted less suspicion in enemy territory, were less likely to be searched and certainly had no fear of being conscripted. In addition they knew how to extract information from German officers that no man could.

The gunning and bravery of the young women was no better displayed than the one who led a cow whose dilated teats were stuffed with microfilm. The German soldiers paid little heed

To the animal but did examine the contents of the young woman's purse.

Because military objectives were constantly changing so was the need for intelligence in various areas.

Near Vesoul a team of six boys and three men scouted the approaches and reported light German presence. The wife of a Vesoul police official walked fifty kilometers through a heavy all night barrage to that city and returned with an overlay of defenses two hours before the assault began. Her report said after speaking with some German soldiers and nuns she learned the town's garrison consisted of twelve men and non-coms billeted at the hospital and four officers and a few more enlisted men at the Kommandantur a few blocks away.

On Sept. 14, 1944 G-2 requested reconnaissance of an area where the FFI had reported the presence of 100 tanks. The lines were once more infiltrated the night preceding an attack and found the report to be false.

At other levels of the societal structure two French girls, forced by the Germans to work in a brothel, volunteered their services in soliciting intelligence. While a third agent sat in a closet with a small table and light recording conversations the girls pried information from the Germans.

LVII
Violette Szabo

She was a slender, beautiful 22 year-old mother whose husband had been killed fighting in North Africa. She grew up a tomboy in London where she outplayed, outran and out shot most of the boys. She joined the SOE and was sent into the Rouen-Channel coastal region prior to D-Day to reconnoiter and also check out SOE agents whose radios had gone silent.

She evaded arrest several times but finally was caught. The Gestapo had surrounded a cottage where she and a French agent were hiding. She persuaded her companion to escape while she covered with his Sten gun. She remained to pick off the Germans from window to window until her ammunition gave out. She was sent to prison in Germany where she was brutally tortured but refused to break. She was shot in January 1945 with two other women couriers at the infamous Nazi prison at Ravensbruck. She was the first British woman to be awarded the George Cross and France's Croix de Guerre.

LVIII
Odette Marie Sansom

She was another SOE heroine. A 34 year-old brunette, mother of three small children, she parachuted into southern France. As she had been born there her language was perfect. Shortly after arranging a large drop to resistance leaders hiding out above Cote d'Azur she was caught. She was tortured brutally but never broke. In one of the unspeakable acts the Germans pulled out her toenails one by one. Still she refused to reveal the name of her fellow parachutist, Peter Churchill. Taken to Ravensbruck she was sentenced to die. Somehow the order was never carried out. At war's end the German commandant of Ravensbruck drove her personally to American lines hoping for clemency. He did not receive it. Sansom was later awarded the George Cross.

LIV
Noor Inayat Khan

An Indian princess, Noor Inayat Khan, worked for SOE. Though born in Russia she lived mostly in France and England. She was proficient as a radio operator which led to her assignment in 1943. She was described as a beautiful but vague and dreamy woman—almost too emotional and sensitive for her dangerous assignment in Versailles. Whether these alleged weaknesses had anything to do with her capture would never be known. Only four months into her mission she was caught, then shot.

LV LVI LVII
Madeleine Damerment—Yolandde Beckman—Elaine Plewman

Also executed with her on the cobblestones of Dachau were Madeleine Damerment, a 27 year old SOE agent from Lille; Swiss born Yolande Beckman, a wireless operator who blew up stretches of railroad between Paris, St. Quentin and Lille for almost a year and Elaine Plewman, part Spanish, part English who was a courier and also an expert in blowing rail tunnels.

LVIII
Yvonne Baseden

Yvonne Baseden, SOE's youngest radio operator, was caught and cruelly tortured at Ravensbruck where upward of 100,000 women had perished. She lived to be repatriated through the Swedish Red Cross.

LIX
Lisa De Baissac—'

Lise de Baissac, 32, entered France using the cover of a poor widow, slightly adelpated, who hunted rock specimens and bird eggs by day on the road from Bordeaux to Paris. At night she directed airborne material drops for the Maquis. She trained recruits in the use of the Sten gun and the manly art of self-defense such as garroting sentries.

LX
Diana Hope Rowden

She was cut off in southern France when the French government surrendered to the Nazis. In a series of harrowing events she escaped through Spain, then Portugal to England. In July 1941 she joined the WAAF and volunteered for intelligence work. She was dropped near Dijon where the French Maquis met her. The Canaris organization picked her up and she was sent to Natzweiler. She was thrown alive into the camps cremation oven.

LXI
Jeannie Rousseau

An example of the importance of those who served on the home front was this woman. She exemplified how painstaking research and analysis can serve. Taking seriously Hitler's threats of a new, secret weapon to change the course of the war she created a brilliant report on what might happen. A graduate of Ecoles des Sciences Politiques she was also fluent in four languages. She first reported on the V-l, a flying bomb. Her next report was on the V-2, a new bomb that could be launched vertically from concrete platforms. Her reports, when coupled with the early spottings of the Peenemunde launching pads by Britain's female operative, Babington-Smith, gave England time to prepare for the attacks before they were launched.

LXII
Isabel Townsend Pell

She was another American woman who elected to remain in occupied France feeling she could get along with the Germans. She became drawn into the conflict and went to work with the underground. One day she came across sixteen American paratroopers who had been dropped ten miles from their target. The area was under absolute German control and they were in extreme danger. She led them to cover, then got them in her own home arranging for their safe return to American lines. She was one of the few American women awarded the Medal of Resistance by the French.

LXIII LXIV
Rosamond Frame—Joy Romer

In 1943 the U.S. Embassy in New Delhi, India faced a problem. Sensitive information was being leaked to China, our supposed ally. It had been determined the Chinese Government was more interested in stockpiling American arms for its eventual fight with the Communists than defeating the Japanese.

An in-house investigation began involving Rosamond Frame and Joy Romer along with Major Oliver Galdwell. After it was completed it revealed two Chinese employees were stealing information and selling it—to the Japanese. They were arrested and incarcerated.

A few weeks later Joy Romer was accosted on the street and brutally beaten. Her injuries were so severe she did not recover and died in the hosital.

OSS felt the attack was done at the direction of Chinese General Tai Li who headed the Secret Police. He most likely resented American intervention in what he considered a Chinese affair.

Rosamond Frame had grown up in China and was fluent in the language. She had thrown elegant parties while in Chungking and helped bridge the cultural gap between Chinese and Americans.

LXV
Marlene Dietrich

The glamorous movie star was desperately sought after by Hitler as a representative of the pure Aryan race. Her fame would have done much to boost the Nazi cause.

She defiantly said she had no sympathy for the Nazi cause, she was an American and would support the Allied effort. She was pressed into service singing American songs to be broadcast to German soldiers to occupy their lonely hours. And also to make them a big nostalgic and home sick.

Included were such songs as, "I've Told Every Little Star", "Is You Is Or Is You Ain't My Baby", "I'll get By' and, "My Heart Stood Still". In some cases the words were slightly altered for propaganda purposes.

At the end of the war someone collected most of her songs and a record was made of the "OSS Songs".

LXVI
Maria Dunaieva Aka The Red Mate Harti

NKVD chief Laurenti Beria could take great pride in this woman's accomplishments· Maria Dunaieva was what the British would term, smashing. A redhead that would turn any mans head she had received her full training in Beria's espionage school.

Her operations began at the period where the American and Russian forces had joined together in the heart of Germany. Fighting still went on as American and Russian bombers hit the oilfields of Baku.

Her mission was simply to seduce as many American soldiers as possible and gather whatever information she could get from them. She quickly worked her way into the soldiers hearts and affection. Her persona was that of an open, honest and loving woman. But it was't necessarily so.

Her first husband, now living in New York, said he was played for a sucker. He felt she truly loved him. When he returned home the Russians refused her an exit visa. He concludes his thoughts by saying, "I still cannot believe she has now married another American soldier without even a divorce. I just don't believe it".

No one seems to know how many other men she might have married but the last one, James McMillin was certainly a prize. His befuddled and heartsick parents reported Maria seemed like a beautiful and honest girl who would have been welcome on their farm.

The State Department notified the parents that their son had married a Soviet spy, renounced his American citizenship, quit the American Embassy and applied for Soviet citizenship. Their son never wrote them.

But this was just the beginning of the damage to America for Maria had first made sure she had a winner and she did. McMillin was a code clerk in the Embassy in Moscow. When he left he took with him all of the current U.S. codes enabling the Soviets to read all past messages they had filed and the few that went through until such time as the codes could be changed.

LXVII
Yvonne De Ridder Files

From her comfortable apartment in Antwerp, Yvonne De Ridder and her husband, Ed, began a retreat from advancing German forces in May of 1940. Ed, being of Jewish descent, although an American, had a very specific reason for fleeing the Germans.

After eight days of confused people wandering the roads they arrived in Poitier, France which had become a gathering place for Belgians fleeing the war. They found a place to stay and remained there until August when they decided to go back to Antwerp.

Luftwaffe personnel had moved into their apartment building making it uncomfortable. Resistance had begun and reprisals in the form of executions were already taking place. It made her feel she must do something for her country.

Her husband decided he must leave and, with German permission, left on the last train to leave for Portugal via France. She worked as a secretary for her father riding her bicycle twenty five minutes daily to his office.

One day she was talking to a stranger in the street. She had a sixth sense he was a member of the resistance. As she left she said, "If I can help you in any way, let me know."

It was an innocent remark but in the double talk the natives used when talking about the occupying forces it struck home. From the way he looked at her she knew she had struck pay dirt.

Two weeks later she received a caller who simply told her she had checked out alright and could begin work. She was now involved. At first she typed out lists of numbers that identified train movements and sometimes their cargo. The reports were relayed to England by a father-son team elsewhere.

Then the day came when a Belgian pilot, shot down, needed to get out of the country. She gladly accepted him in her apartment and received instructions to take him to Brussels where another contact would take over. The 34 minute train ride was tense as the fear his papers might be checked at any time by roving Gestapo agents could undo both of them. They were lucky.

She kept her intelligence work a secret, even from her father. For anyone to know would be dangerous for them should she ever be caught.

For eighteen months the espionage unit she was a part of continued its broadcasts to England. Then disaster! The home of the father-son broadcast center was raided. The father was killed but the son did escape. It was evident there was an informer. The entire unit shut down and began an internal examination.

The resistance was picking up and German reactions were quick and severe. July 21, 1941 was Belgian National

Day and the flying of the Belgian flag was strictly ver-
boten. In a show of defiance Yvonne and her friend
dressed in the national colors and sent into the streets.
She wore a red blouse, black skirt and yellow belt. The
Belgians smiled and secretly clasped their hands in
appreciation. Nothing came of it as the Germans chose to
ignore the statement of the two women.

Two months after the shutdown of the unit one of its
members appeared at her door. Would she like to go
back to work? "Of course", she replied enthusiastically.

When told her new job would be sabotage she didn't
flinch. Her living/dining room became a center for
bomb production. Though not a chemist she learned the
fine art of hot needles, sugar, fuses and use of sulphur.
She lined the bombs up on the keyboard of her piano.

Another device was a V-shaped tire destroyer. Put
under the wheel of a military vehicle its upright prong
penetrated the rubber as the base broke off. It
immediately punctured the tire and by the time the
driver realized it was flat he had totally destroyed the tire.
In rubber short Germany it created a big problem. She
placed many of these with great anxiety. Anyone bending
over near a military vehicle was immediately suspect.

Her apartment had now been designated as a sub-
depot for arms and material shipment. Large
shipments of chemicals were arriving in metal drums.
The English had been dropping them. She had to store
them in the basement of her building. A nosy
neighbor gave her problems.

One day he talked to her about the various men coming and going from her apartment. He naturally
assumed she was a prostitute. She asked him if he was

paying her rent and, since he wasn't, would he please leave her alone. But on many occasions she caught him snooping and certainly didn't want it known what she was really up to.

Bombing raids that flew over Belgium were increasing daily. Also the crews that were shot down and needed shelter increased. She took one into her apartment until he could be called for. Then another and finally at one time she had five airmen in her care. And then one morning, the inevitable. A breathless young member of the resistance appeared at her door with the words she dreaded to hear.

"Get out. You have been betrayed. They'll be here in an hour."

She knew the penalty was death all along and now zero hour was here.

The timing couldn't have been worse. She still had the five airmen in her apartment and told them. Nervously they peered from the window and observed small groups of people sitting on benches where they had never been. It was obvious the Gestapo was waiting.

Two days passed with the waiting game going on. The Gestapo was waiting to catch more fish in their net.

Finally, Donald, another resistance worker, came to her door. He brought a huge bouquet of roses. She told him of her plight and he arranged to sneak the airmen out.

(Later it turned out Donald was her betrayer. His red roses were a signal to the Gestapo to let the airmen leave. He was caught after the war and executed. He freely admitted to betraying 75 people for his fee of 1,000 marks each).

When others finally arranged to sneak her out she was taken to the home of a Mrs. V who put her up. She continued her work with airmen and got several more out safely.

One morning she answered a knock at the door. She opened it and was asked if she was Madame Yvonne. She said she was. The man in civilian clothes snapped the handcuffs on her, said she was under arrest and took her away.

Her prison was a large mansion requisitioned by the Germans—the local SS headquarters. It was known as 'Torture House'.

To her interrogators she said she knew nothing. She denied and denied. A short time later the kid gloves came off and she was dealt a backhand time and again knocking her out of her chair. Still she knew nothing. When confronted with a stick of explosive charge they had taken from her apartment she concocted the story she thought it was putty.

The backhands turned into whippings. In a rage she was beat so badly on her arms and legs that her legs turned purple. When a German matron took her to see the doctor, so ugly were her wounds, he asked who had done this to her.

The Matron replied it was the Secret Field Police to which the doctor replied then he could do nothing. They were untouchable.

After that incident she was told she would be executed in six weeks. And it would be by hanging, a fate reserved for resistance and espionage workers.

Her questioning and beating continued. The weeks slipped by. And then one day, ten days before her execution date, her door was opened and the matron told her to go home. She couldn't believe it but she wasted no time. She stopped at the desk to collect her pathetic belongs they had taken when she arrived, then hit the streets. It was 6 p.m. and dark already. She was not in a good section of the town but managed to reach her uncle's place where she learned her father had been killed.

Back in her ransacked apartment she heard shots and, together with neighbors, watched as British soldiers fought their way onto the street and finally drove the Germans out. There were wild celebrations.

She later came to America. For her heroic work she was decorated by the British, Belgian and French governments and received a special certificate signed by General Dwight Elsenhower, a total of 7 medals. In 1950 she appeared on 'THIS IS YOUR LIFE' hosted by Ralph Edwards. She was honored on national television's LIFE channel on August 4, 1996. The one-hour program documented Allied female spies calling attention to their patriotism, courage and unwavering determination.

In 1963 her divorce, started two years earlier, was granted. She married Lt. Col. Roger Files, an American fighter pilot. They now live in Riverside, Calif.

LXVIII
Marie

She was a strikingly beautiful Alsatian woman working as a maid for Herr von Felsek. She had become his mistress a year ago and he was well pleased with what she brought into his life.

von Felsek was an author of several successful books. He was well known to the homicide squad for he was sure to turn up at every murder. He brought with him several bottles of brandy that assured him some special information for future stories.

He had an interesting background. Immediately after World War I he had escaped from a Russian prisoner of war camp. His records in the Weimer Republic showed he had been a counter-espionage officer.

The peace in the household was broken all too often by a low flying advertising plane. It annoyed Marie as well as Felsek because it seemed to fly constantly. On occasion it would drop some small advertising trinket or sky-write a message.

But a more worrisome event came one day in the form of two visitors .

Marie came in with a concerned look. Two men were there to see Felsek. This was the time of growing concern over loss of freedoms to the Nazi party.

The two men handed identification showing them to be Gestapo officers. Felsek felt no fear—his record was above reproach. Their records showed he had been a counterespionage agent some years back and they were interested in him. The Gestapo, they explained, was forming its own counter-espionage unit in addition to that of the Wehrmacht. They felt his talents could well serve them in this capacity.

Felsek had never expected this. As a member of a prominent German family he had only contempt for the Gestapo and its Nazi parent. He stammered, then said he didn't know if he was suited and asked for time to think it over.

They agreed and left.

His concern over the proposition was not helped by the irritating low flying plane. He shook his fist at it, then went to a cafe to think it over.

He delayed several weeks but the ever-persistent Gestapo finally made it clear to him. He had better do it.

Finally he agreed and was moved into his office in the Prinz Albrecht-strasse. He told himself it was only honorary. Since he disliked his bosses and what they stood for it was only understandable he did little work. He simply put in his time.

Marie consoled him and well understood his position. She, too, feared and hated the Gestapo.

One day an incident happened he knew was bound to come. His superiors called him in to complain about his lack of results. In essence he was told to shape up.

Back at his desk his thoughts were interrupted once more by the plane. He was seeking something that would get them off his back and came to a decision. Aerial photography was more and more in use as a military intelligence tool and he drafted a memo. In it he questioned why a private plane should be allowed to fly all over the area and why there was no investigation of the occupants of any such plane. He sent it in hoping it would buy him some time.

He got an immediate reply. It was not pleasant.

The Air Ministry coldly informed him the pilot was one of Germany's top pilots from the first World War. He had been decorated for his courage and was above reproach. How dare anyone even consider questioning his patriotism.

To emphasize his point the Air Ministry ordered the plane be brought down at Staaken airfield. Felsek was ordered to go along for this humiliating showdown.

At the airfield soldiers with carbines stood at the ready. The advertising plane came in shepherded by three swift fighter planes that had been ordered to bring it in.

The plane rolled to a stop. The soldiers formed a circle around it. The pilot stepped out, took in the scene, then casually leaned against the plane and lit a cigarette.

"You see.».you see this man. He is the famous pilot Rheinfeld," Felsek was told.

Rheinfeld walked over to the officers and stunned them when he said, "1 was misled". Everyone stood dumbfounded.

An investigation revealed a built in camera. The other occupant of the plane was a mechanic—and he was French, not German. Rheinfeld was so traumatized he could hardly get his arms behind his back for the handcuffs. The Frenchman willingly, almost gleefully held out his wrists and confessed all. He said there would be no use in denying what he had been about. He added he had been doing this type of work around Germany for some time and all his work had already been forwarded to his superiors. He expected a death sentence.

The Gestapo was gleeful. They had picked up the most important spy against the Third Reich to date and not the military counter-espionage branch.

That night Felsek sat quietly thinking over the day's events. The doorbell rang. He assumed some other Gestapo agents were coming to share their joy with him.

He got a shock. An air officer and two soldiers placed him under arrest for suspicion of espionage.

The next morning they played their cards. "How did you know there was a spy in that plane?, they demanded.

"I didn't know", was all he could reply. They then asked about Marie and again he offered nothing."

By now the Gestapo learned of his arrest and ordered his release. They charged departmental jealousy. Several days later Felsek and Marie were in Sweden being interviewed by author, Kurt Singer. She was lovely in a silver lame dress. They had just been married.

Felsek confessed he knew of the spy only because of Marie. She appeared to be the sparkplug of the operation. She had told him. France had sent her to spy on Felsek but the two had fallen in love. They worked together. With the Gestapo putting pressure on Felsek they had to do something.

Singer pointed out they had bought their freedom with the death of the two airmen.

Again Marie spoke.

"No, it was actually easy. I knew we had in France two German agents who also had had the same kind of bad luck. We'd put them on ice. After the Berlin affair they were exchanged so no one was executed. If it were wartime that probably wouldn't have happened. But in peace time such deals occurs fairly often."

The last thing heard from them was a card from Germany in 1948. They were on their way to Shanghai.

CHAPTER 8

▼

LXIX
MARIA GULEVIC

Czechoslovakia presented considerable problems to the resistance and OSS in particular. It was through the Czech Government-in-Exile they made arrangements to infiltrate a liaison group and an air crew rescue unit. The Slovak army and partisans prepared the Tri Duby airfield for B-17 landings and arranged recognition signals•

In September and October 1944 B-17s flew in five tons of military supplies, 22 OSS agents and flew out 43 downed airmen. A stream of intelligence on German units and activities followed. The Germans could not risk continued sabotage in their area and in September began a systematic drive to wipe out all resistance. As the noose tightened the resistance became increasingly disorganized and fled taking weapons and supplies with them. They headed toward the Russian lines.

With severe winter hitting the OSS men and newly downed airmen the situation became critical.

At this point a young schoolteacher in the village of Hrnova, Maria Gulevic, became involved.

She had never intended to get involved, she said. When approached by her brother to take a Jewish mother and her son "for just a few days until she can find another place", she agreed. She hid them from April 1944 to the following July. Then she found a way to move them to a safer place in the mountains. But while she was hiding them someone reported her to the authorities. Luckily the person sent to investigate her was also working with the underground, which saved her life.

She carried intelligence information from her little village to Bratislava. This hazardous doing almost ended her brief career. On a train trip the Gestapo stopped her train and proceeded to check the passengers luggage. Maria happened to be carrying a short wave radio, a sure death sentence.

Fate intervened in the form of some German soldiers in a compartment who began flirting with her. She gladly returned their glad eye.

"Fraulein, why don't you join us", one asked. They made a seat for her and one of them even carried her suitcase into the compartment.

The Gestapo walked by, saluted, and continued on checking the other passengers.

With this bit of activity she was next to become involved as a courier for the European underground. Finally she began serving as a guide to those refugees and OSS agents trying to get out of what was then Slovakia.

At the time she spoke Russian, Hungarian, Slovak and some English. She ran into several dozen OSS agents desperate to get away from the oncoming Germans. They headed into the mountains with her as their guide.

The suffering was incredible for several months near the end of 1944. She moved them from place to place almost nightly, often using relatives for advice and shelter. Along with the agents she suffered lice and frostbite. Her right foot was so frostbitten her people begged her to go to a hospital. She refused knowing she would never come out as the Germans had her name by now.

In December she went with two Americans and two British to an inn where an airdrop was expected. The rest of their group stayed behind at a small hunting lodge.

When they returned the lodge had been raided by the Germans. All were taken away and executed.

The weather proved even more cruel than the Germans. On one day 83 Czech partisans, waiting for the return of a reconnaissance patrol, died of cold.

In some fashion the balance of OSS men and many airmen managed to reunite. But one by one they died off traversing the mountains. Maria went in and out of enemy lines bringing what food, medicine and bandages she could sneak through. She gave encouragement to those men who were now totally dependent on her.

On 6 November one OSS member and five American aviators on patrol were captured.

On 11 November all the airmen, together with two OSS officers, elected to stop in a village and surrender. In twos and threes others were picked up by the Germans, often betrayed by the partisans.

At Christmas the remaining OSS agents were staying at a mountain hotel ner Veiny Bok. On 26 December 250 Germans and Hlinka guards attacked the hotel and captured them.

All were taken to the infamous Mauthausen concentration camp and tortured. On 22 January 1945 they were all executed. Maria and two OSS agents who had been out, survived. They escaped by hiking over 50 miles to the Russian lines.

She eventually came to America and accepted a scholarship at Vassar. While there she worked in the kitchen. Her first night she broke down and cried when she saw the food being thrown out. The memory of starving people, her family included, was too much for her.

She was awarded the Bronze Star in a West Point ceremony in May 1946.

Many airmen and OSS agents owe their lives to this woman. She is now a realtor and lives in Oxnard, California.

LXVIII
Kiyomi

A cat and mouse game was being played out in Tokyo in the late 1930s.

The Kempei Tai, Japanese counterintelligence, was aware of Soviet espionage and began narrowing down the suspects. Colonel Osaki who headed the Kempei Tai concentrated on Richard Sorge, a hard drinking womanizer whose cover was that of a journalist. He was an avowed Communist under direction of Moscow with the mission of determining if Japan was going to attack Russia.

Sorge was considered by many in later years as one of the greatest spies to practice that trade.

Knowing of his strong sex drive Osaki invited Sorge to join him at the Fuji Club where he would meet a beautiful new entertainer, Kiyomi.

He watched her perform the rice dance in which the face is hidden but not the body. He was immediately enthralled. Night after night he returned to the Fuji Club. He sent numerous notes and gifts.

She tore up his notes and sent his gifts back.

When he failed to appear one night she realized she had gone too far in her game of tantalizing him. She talked with Osaki, her controller, and told him of the problem.

Before she had concluded her performance that night Sorge was on hand. She went out with him afterwards. He took her to bed and she became his mistress.

Several nights later the sharp-eyed Kiyomi noticed a waiter drop a note on Sorge's table. It was from one of his agents, Miyagi, who warned him he was under surveillance by the Japanese.

The next night she saw another note being dropped at his table. She knew it was essential she get the note and invited him to her dressing room right after her last dance. He would still have the note with him she rationalized.

She did not let him out of her sight. He said he had rented a room for the, night and they headed for it. The highly sexed Sorge could not even wait till they reached the room. He stopped the car along the way and seduced her. At the same time he tore the note up and threw the pieces out the window.

Thinking quickly Kiyomi asked him to stop at the next call box. She wanted to phone her mother to tell her she was going to spend the night with a girl friend.

As Sorge sat in the car she called Osaki to tell him of the torn note, then returned to the car.

When they reached the Villa he excused himself and went down to the beach. There he met another member of his ring and gave him two messages. The first was that a Japanese carrier fleet would attack Pearl Harbor probably on November 6th. The second was that their unit was compromised and was being disbanded.

Returning to the villa he was served a dinner prepared Japanese style by Kiyomi. Then, true to fashion, he took her to bed once more.

Osaki's men had retrieved and reconstructed the torn up note. It gave them all they needed to indict Sorge and his confederates. On October 15, 1941 Osaki and two of his men called on Sorge. They bowed, then simply handed him the note now pasted together. Sorge realized immediately Kiyomi had betrayed him. He didn't bother to look at her but simply walked out with Osaki.

The trial was held on September 29, 1943. Sorge attempted to exonerate his confederates by taking full responsibility. He was given the death penalty.

Negotiations were still in the air as Japan tried to obtain a peace pact with the Soviet Union. They offered Sorge as a pawn but it was turned down.

It was reported he was executed on the anniversary of the Soviet resolution as a result of the failed peace negotiations.

Kiyomi was assassinated three years later as she left her club. It appeared to be a classic SMERSH hit as the Soviets avenged the death of one of their greatest spies.

LXXI
Barbara Issikides

The concert pianist, Barbara Issikides, took her bow to thunderous applause in Zurich in late 1943. She appeared tall and elegant, a white streak coursing through her dark hair. Following the concert she went to the luxurious apartment of industrialist, Kurt Grimm in the Hotel Bellerive au Lac.

She and Grimm were part of a 14 member anti-Nazi group. Though apolitical she had become enamored with the idealism of Grimm and a leftist priest, Henrich Maier who enjoined her with this small group. She greatly admired their intellect and shared a deep hatred of the Nazis.

Grimm supplied valuable information to Allen Dulles in his OSS office. While not engaged in actual espionage Barbara was able to contribute in her own unique way.

She was Viennese and not quite aged thirty. Her father was a prosperous rug merchant in Vienna and a leader in that city's Greek community. As a concert pianist she traveled easily in countries the Nazis controlled.

After concerts she would mingle with many of the Nazis and encourage them as they tried to impress her with their importance and might. Possessed with a retentive mind she would then transfer the information on to her Zurich base.

Her group had contacts in Istanbul and had brief talks with OSS Turkey. Allen Dulles told them to beware of these Istanbul agents. His advice, sadly, proved sound.

There were seventeen foreign intelligence services within Istanbul. The OSS mission had a Czech engineer, code named DOGWOOD. He was somewhat questionable having been passed along by the British. He refused to give his contacts but provided a steady stream of information. The OSS Chief made the mistake of not insisting on meeting his contacts in order to more properly evaluate his information.

A Hungarian agent contacted DOGWOOD suggesting they might cooperate in their missions. DOGWOOD, taking it upon himself to handle the agent personally, shared with him information on those agents working in Austria and Hungary.

On March 19, 1944, Germany invaded Hungary and picked up their security files. Included were the names of several of the Zurich group of 14 including Barbara Issikides. Within twelve days they were arrested in Vienna.

In late 1944 two of the Zurich group, the leftist priest and the industrialist, were tried in a Federal Court in Vienna. Charged with fomenting a separatist movement and giving information to the enemy they were sentenced to death.

While she was not tortured Barbara Issikides was subjected to near inhumane interrogation. Time and again she revealed nothing, which infuriated her Gestapo captors. She managed to concentrate on other subjects and did not let them penetrate her mind. At one point a special pencil used to hide messages was put before her. "You know what this is", they shouted. She shook her head. Months of constant interrogation weakened her but her spirit never sagged. They respected her as a concert artist but daily saw her losing weight and strength.

Several months later she complained of severe stomach pains. Taken to a hospital she was treated by Dr. Franke in Vienna. Recognizing her as the artist he also was aware she was an accomplished actress. Going along with her he diagnosed a duodenal ulcer and put her in a hospital. The four weeks he was able to keep her there were sufficient to forestall her trial letting her survive.

At the end of the four weeks the Allies arrived and she was freed. The priest and industrialist were executed the last week before they would have been freed, however.

With her strength returning she gave another concert in Zurich followed by a lavish OSS reception afterwards. But the ordeal had taken a toll. Exhausted, she finally gave up her career and settled down in marriage.

LXXII LXXIII
Ann and Judd Kappius—Hilde Meisel

Area 0 was a beautiful English manor outside London which OSS used as a staging area. Late in September 1944 an OSS officer was given the job of escorting two women agents to Switzerland. They were to then infiltrate Germany and join with Jupp Kappius, the OSS agent in Bocus and husband of Anne Kappius.

The other woman was Hilde Meisel who had been thrown together in OSS work with Arthur Goldberg in London. She was to go to Vienna and set up a group of other radical socialists. Her codename was CROCUS.

Their plane landed in the small French town of Thonon on the Lake Geneva shores. After dinner in the home of a host they departed for their missions the next day.

Anne Kappius was to act as a courier for her husband in addition to gathering intelligence. Jupp Kappius had been instrumental in developing extremely good intelligence. In addition he had established cadres throughout Bochum, Essen, Witten and other cities in the Ruhr.

Among other intelligence was the fact life in the Ruhr was normal. The people ate well, trains and buses ran on schedule, factories and stores hummed. It was a startling revelation to him. He reported it and shortly bombers changed it all as they destroyed large parts of the area shutting off power and disrupting what had been a normal life.

OSS wanted to supply him with a radio and operator. He refused it saying he would rely on his wife as courier. She did deliver his reports into Switzerland, then return. Her cover was that of a nurse.

Hilde Meisel entered Austria in the spring of 1945. She set up a chain of socialist sympathizers. She returned to the border preparatory to entering Switzerland where she ran into an SS patrol. A shot from one of their rifles shattered both of her legs. Before they could capture her she bit into her 'L' pill, a cyanide capsule. Death came immediately.

Judd and Anne Kappius survived the war and returned to Germany. He was later elected to the state legislature of North Rhine-Westphalia.

LXXIV
Lily Sergueiev Aka Tramp

As in all military camps and in all wars there are the camp followers—prostitutes. Every nation has had and will have these women eager to ply their trade.

Many of them sought the role of spies to augment their income, some for the sense of adventure and some out of sheer patriotism.

Lily Sergueiev was the latter. She was of Russian parents but lived in France and plied her trade as a lady of the night.

In 1932 she was introduced to Felix Dassel who did recruiting for the Abwehr• He remained in her mind although it is not known if they kept in contact after that.

When the Germans involved Poland in 1939 she was in France and knew France would soon be involved. She kept a diary. An entry on December 20, 1940, advised she had been lying in her bed and the thought of becoming an agent suddenly came to her.

She got back in touch with Dassel and asked to be put in touch with the German secret service. He arranged a meeting for her with Major Emil Kleimann who was second in command in Paris.

He fell for this attractive girl and soon was escorting her to all the finest night spots in Paris. He was indeed interested in her working for Germany. She was given the codename, TRAMP.

Her loyalty never was in question for her plan was to enter England as an Abwehr agent, then work as a double agent for the Allies.

In 1943 she was authorized by Kleinmann to go to England through Spain. In Madrid she contacted British intelligence and told them her story. They got her to England where she was interviewed by MI5 and immediately went to work with them. She transmitted that information the British fed her using some true facts to satisfy the Germans. The Germans seemed satisfied she was all she said she was.

In March 1944 she lured Kleinmann to Lisbon saying she needed her own transmitter. It was taking her too long to transmit. He was easy prey and saw to it that she had it immediately.

Lily was the only female agent to have her own secret radio and used it to broadcast false information to keep the Germans off guard. She became extremely important to the Allies plans of sending false information about the pending invasion of Normandy. MI5 declared she was the single most important cog in the Allies plans to convince the Germans there would be no invasion at Normandy.

An entry in her diary July 1, 1944, just after the Normandy landing read, "I'm number 75.034. I've lost my personality. With it I've lost my solitary state. I'm no longer alone. I've got the whole army with me".

Many an Allied soldier who ordinarily would not have lived through the war, did so because of this one woman's cleverness and loyalty.

LXXV
Ursula Ruth Kuczynski Aka Sonja

Some agents endured for decades. A perfect example of this was Ursula Ruth Kuczynski. So long was her service and hard to track that to date it is difficult to evaluate her effectiveness.

Her father, a German Jew, taught economics at Oxford University. Around 1926 she went to New York City. She found employment in a book store and there met Rudolph Hamburger. He was about to finish his studies to become an architect.

They dated, then she returned to Germany. He followed and in 1929 they were married.

She had become an ardent Communist. His politics were to the left but not to the degree of his wife.

In 1930 he took an assignment in Shanghai and she followed. Here her path crossed with Agnes Smedley who, together with her leader, Richard Sorge, convinced her to enter the field of espionage. She was given the code name of Sonja.

For whatever reasons she did not tell her husband. Their flat was used as a meeting place.

He must have felt it strange when she was called to Moscow for training. When she returned she moved to Mukden. She left China in 1935. Her husband was not with her.

From there she headed back to Russia for more training in their radio operators school, then returned to England to see her parents.

To further tie their agents to them the Russians gave her rank in their KGB organization. She was made a lieutenant-colonel.

In England she settled down after making contact with her controller. Two Britons were made known to her who were to assist her in a new mission she was to take in Switzerland.

Her next home was in Montreux. 'Allen', actually Alexander Foote, was assigned as her radio operator.

Although the parentage is not clear she had two children by this time. It had no effect on her espionage work, however.

In 1939 she met another man she called Len. A strong suggestion was received from Moscow that she should divorce her first husband and marry Len for the sole purpose of getting him a British passport.

In spite of the wartime restrictions on traveling she managed to get to England where she and Len (actually Leon Buerton) settled down in a rented house near Oxford.

During this period she was transmitting to Russia several times a week.

Through an RAF contact she was updated on the latest aeronautical information. She was also helped in her work by her father and strangely enough by her brother, Jurgen, a Colonel in the U.S. Army who also did some work with the OSS.

Her former radio operator, Foote, left Russia and went to British Intelligence to tell them of Sonja and Len.

Both were interrogated by the British but strangely chose to practically ignore her. It appears there was collusion within British ranks.

Sonja and Len took a brief trip to East Berlin and never returned.

LXXVI
Vera

Three missions were sent into Italy in December 1943 and January 1944. They were CASSANO, MARIA

GIOVANNA and NADA. CASSANO landed safely and continued operations until May 1944 when they were uncovered by the Germans who killed two of them and a passerby. The radio operator escaped.

The MARIO GIOVANNA team transmitted successfully for a month and was ordered into Genoa. At the railroad station a customs officer insisted on inspecting the luggage containing the team's radio set. As he seized it the agent shot him. In the confusion the agent escaped. The team operated until September 1944 when the Germans uncovered them killing two and took over the radio as a deception.

The key member of NADA was a woman only known as 'Vera'. Vera carried a radio set in a suitcase to the leader of the Tuscan resistance movement. It was a 200 mile trip and extremely hazardous in view of the spot checks on train by soldiers. After the sets delivery she established contact with guerrilla groups in the Spezia area and with the CLN in Florence. Through her efforts 65 supply operations by parachute were arranged and safely dropped.

Her group warned her one of her radio operators was suspect. He lived with a German chorus girl and was in the pay of the German SS. In addition he had a loose mouth and was heard boasting in public of his radio and cipher work.

Feeling they had enough evidence the members of the resistance abducted the man and executed him.

Because of the OSS supplies Vera had brought to one resistance group the partisans were able to be of immediate assistance to the U.S. forces. As an example an enemy staff car carrying Japanese military and naval attaches was demolished at a roadblock. Highly classified papers were taken from the bodies and brought to OSS. When American troops entered Florence the operations of this group alone accounted for some 500 German casualties and the blowing of seven major highway and railroad bridges impeding the German retreat.

On July 2, 1944, while Vera and her operator were in contact with her OSS base the Germans burst into the room. A fierce fight ensued. Vera, using hand grenades, killed the German major and two of his soldiers. Before escaping out of the window she succeeded in destroying the radio. They joined a patriot group a short distance outside of Florence. Within eight days she found means of reopening communications with OSS. By September she had a price on her causing her to escape. She crossed into American lines during an artillery battle.

She survived the war and quickly blended back into the fabric from which she had come.

LXXVII
Marjorie Switz

A Soviet spy ring was confounding the French Deuxieme Bureau in 1943. Some small time operators had been picked up with vital information being conveyed to the Soviets. But the natural desire was to find the ringleaders and break up the operation.

It began with a few strands of blonde hair that had adhered to a roll of camera film and wound up in the Deuxieme Bureau. This was the first hint they had of a woman since the hair proved to be from a female.

With this thin lead the French worked together with the British and Americans to eventually break up a group that operated throughout America, Asia, Europe and even Africa. Thoroughly opportunistic the group even sold Nazi secrets to Poland and Yugoslavia. The members had been told to join Fascist groups in order to benefit from their secrets.

They soon wound up on the payroll of Admiral Walter Canaris, head of the German Intelligence Service.

Heading the spy group was Marjorie Switz who was dedicated to the Bolshevist cause. She had an excellent working knowledge of mechanized war weapons. She talked convincingly of secret rays or super range finders that could detect aircraft many miles away. Some of those who accepted everything she said at face value became convinced she knew of a death ray. Those more versed in warfare knew it had to be radar.

The Switz group made numerous attempts to infiltrate the British and get an idea of their coastal warning system. Fortunately the British were old hands at counterespionage and kept their secrets to themselves.

Backing the Switz group all the way was a mastermind with unlimited Soviet funds working under the cover of a commercial organization. It had branches in London, Paris, Brussels, Stockholm and Berlin.

Second in command of the group was Robert Switz, her husband. He had been dismissed from the American Air Corps.

Also working with them was German-born Baroness Lydia Stahl and two Soviet citizens, Benjamin Bercovitz and Boris Rashevsky. The Baroness was all too well known as a Nazi agent. When caught she was sentenced to five years for working both sides of the fence. She had sold information to both the Soviets and Nazis.

A strong, free wheeling woman, Marjorie Switz headed what was unofficially the group's Board of Directors. Her subservient husband took orders from her along with the others.

She picked up a French Colonel who made love to her, a famous explosive expert in need of money and a biologist engaged at the Sorbonne. Each had his own specialty and was expected to add to the overall picture.

She also had imagination. Agents needed places to secrete their messages or materials. She envisioned something special and hired Dr. Riva Davocici, a Rumanian dentist, to fit the couriers' mouths with hollow gold teeth. They were suitable for concealing onion-skin paper copies of documents.

From dentistry she turned to music and formed her own small orchestra. It toured Europe with its wind instruments crammed with documents. To get information out of London she created a secret pocket in a volume of Lloyd George's memoirs.

During all this activity the Switz's lived quite comfortably in their apartment in Chelsea.

A few of their agents were picked up and encouraged to tell all for leniency. They agreed and slowly the organizational structure and its leaders were uncovered. The gang was finally broken, its leaders incarcerated.

LXXVIII
Kristina Skarbek

Good agents come from all walks of life. Such was Countess Kristina Gizycki Skarbek, daughter of a distinguished Polish family.

Tall, elegant and exceedingly attractive she became 'Miss Poland' in her early teens. In a highly fashionable wedding she married a man from a wealthy home. For reasons unknown it lasted only a few weeks.

She then married George Gizycki, a man twenty years her senior. His work took them to Addis Ababa and while there WW11 broke out.

The adventurous Kristina traveled to England and offered her services to British Intelligence. Her beauty, charm and spirit to say nothing of the many languages she spoke, convinced them and she was accepted for training.

She changed her name to the easier Christine Granville. Under cover as a journalist she was sent to Budapest. She went back and forth into Poland to smuggle out Allied officers and fellow countrymen.

On one of the missions into Poland she was detained, questioned and then put under arrest. She managed to escape but, undeterred, went back.

On one of the return trips she was arrested at the Yugoslav border where she had just smuggled four pilots through. Using her wiles she convinced the guards she was just on a picnic. Her car had actually stalled which drew their attention. She talked them into helping her start her car, waved in appreciation and drove away.

During the course of her work she linked up with a Polish cavalry officer, Andrew Kowerski, who helped her. He became a British agent also using the name of Andrew Kennedy.

Fortune smiled on Kristina on many of her missions. From Cairo she became the first female parachutist in the mid-east. It gave her good training for eventual missions into France.

The British had her jump into the Vercors Plateau in Southern France. She worked with both the French Resistance and Italian Partisans operating as a Hockey network courier.

During this time she was listed under the British WAAF with the codename of Pauline.

One time she had been captured by the Germans and escaped down the ski slopes in a hail of machine gun bullets. A second time she was arrested and showed her resourcefulness by biting on her tongue till it bled profusely. Convincing her German captors she had advanced tuberculosis she was placed in a hospital from which she easily escaped.

At one point near the end of the war she heard the Germans were planning to execute two British agents the next day. She went back into their headquarters and said she knew of their plans to execute the British. Pointing out the American forces were not far behind her she struck a bargain. Release the agents to her and she would put in a good word for them with the Americans. If not she would see they burned.

It worked. As she and the agents disappeared the Germans learned, too late, the American forces were not that close.

Lieutenant—Colonel Francois Cammaerts who was headmaster of the Alleyn's School in London, and under whom Kristina had trained, said at war's end, "Kristina was perhaps the greatest person I have ever known."

As the war ended Kristina found herself ignored by the British. She was dismissed with two months salary and forced to find work where she could.

She took employment as a stewardess on a liner. On that ship she met a fellow employee who also worked as a steward. He fell head over heels in love with her but it was not returned.

In a fit of jealousy this woman who had survived capture and some torture ironically lost her life through repeated stabbings by the rejected suitor.

A hint of some scandal remained, however. She said she had evidence that the death of Polish General Sikorski in a plane crash was actually sabotage. Some wonder if the evidence might have been the cause of such poor treatment by the British.

LXXIX
Ilona

She is beautiful, outspoken and too well known in the entertainment world to use her real name at her request. I met her over twenty years ago and have worked with her over those two decades. She will therefore be called Ilona.

Her story begins in the years prior to WWII. Living in eastern Europe she was part of a shattered home. Her father, a respected businessman, committed suicide when she was five years old. Her mother soon remarried a man who had been a close family friend and had been to their home many times.

Ilona was sent to a private school near Paris. She was wise beyond her years. She made the two-day train trip by herself. The war clouds were gathering and lowering during those 1939 times. She found German soldiers also traveling on the train.

For the journey the family maid had packed a lunch which Ilona held in her lap. It had a sandwich of coarse brown bread, some fruit and cookies. After several hours had passed the passengers broke out their lunches and began eating. Ilona waited for a few minutes then opened her sack and removed her food.

The Germans, sitting opposite her, had no food and looked around enviously. Finally one reached across the compartment and simply took her food. He shared it with a companion as Ilona looked on. She was getting her first experience in dealing with the Nazis.

Arriving, hungry, in the Paris station, she was met by someone from the school. She got some food and was taken to her school. Soon after her arrival and involvement in her school work the German invasion of Poland began. War was declared and the people went into their war mode.

When the invasion of France began there was considerable concern over whether or not the Maginot line would hold. There was uneasiness within the school but the teachers kept classes on schedule and tried to ease the students' fears.

The Germans easily breached the Maginot line and did an end around run to overrun France. As their armies neared Paris Ilona was sent to another private school to the south and near the coast. It was in the designated Free France area. The Germans agreed to not occupy the entire country.

The students did their best to continue with their studies as news of problems with the Germans in occupied France came in. How long would they remain unoccupied was the big question.

It was answered when Germany announced it was now going to occupy the entire country. German troops soon arrived in the little town and established a Gestapo headquarters.

One day two Gestapo officers walked into their classroom. They were seeking someone who read and spoke German. Ilona, who spoke German and several other languages, raised her hand.

She was told at the end of her class to report to the Gestapo headquarters.

When she did so she learned why they wanted her. They needed an interpreter. Letters were being received in French that were denouncing French citizens and the Germans, unable to read them, wanted someone to translate them into German.

Ilona was shocked one French citizen would denounce a fellow citizen but soon realized many were seeking special favors from their conquerors while others were simply out for revenge.

It was a distasteful task for a young girl. The Germans treated her kindly but her first brush with them on the train told her what kind of people they were.

Dutifully she took the letters from one basket, rewrote them in German and put them in another basket. She hated it.

She was questioned by her classmates and teacher as to just what went on in the hated Gestapo headquarters. She could only tell them the truth.

Her teacher called her aside one day and revealed a secret. She was with the French underground and they were concerned over those damning letters. Could she in some way see they were lost? She replied the

Germans would know if some disappeared and she would be in trouble.

Finally a plan was worked out through her teacher. When Ilona got a letter denouncing someone she would put it in her purse and take it to her room that night. An underground worker would come, read the letter and then warn the target so he or she might disappear immediately. The next day Ilona would translate the letter and put it in the box. When she had such a letter her signal to the underground would be the angle at which she parked her bicycle outside her room.

There was a definite pattern of those accused departing just before the arrival of the Gestapo but they did not figure it out until one day when Ilona took sick.

She had done her afternoon's work and gone home. In her purse was a letter of condemnation for the town doctor who she knew personally as he had treated her at one time. In the letter the doctor was accused of going into the woods nightly to treat wounded Maquis. She had planned, as usual, to let the underground worker get the information and notify the doctor in time.

She was hungry and opened a can of mushrooms which were tainted. She got the hives and her eyes swelled shut. She became room confined. The Gestapo officer she worked with visited her and, in the course of that visit, opened her purse. He found the letter and soon realized where the leak was coming from.

Through a stroke of luck the doctor was alerted to the letter anyway and did manage to flee that same night.

She was given a stern lecture and sent to a Gestapo prison. It was actually a large villa they had confiscated. Her 'cell' was a large barren room occupied by 39 other women. Some were prostitutes, some common criminals or thieves and others were in for political reasons such as Ilona. From some of the street-hardened women she learned tricks such as scraping tartar from the teeth and putting it in the eye to fake a horrible eye disease and get hospital treatment. The food was abominable. It consisted of beans that contained worms and mildewed bread. When the Quakers got permission to bring in some soap for the women they were so hungry they ate it.

The only item in the large room was a bucket which was their toilet. They took turns emptying it. Ilona who hated the job as much as anyone soon found a way to get out of it. She used the Sherehazade ploy of story telling to while away the boring hours. Anxious for anything to help them escape their surroundings the women agreed she would be relieved of the bucket chore and assembled nightly to hear her tales.

She organized competition in the killing of fleas and lice which abounded. It kept the women busy and gave them a spirit of competition. In short order the now thirteen year-old girl was running the cell.

As the months went by news reached them of an Allied invasion. The llth Panzer Division from her area was called north to reinforce German positions. Suddenly the little town was free. The prison doors were opened and she was free after 69 days in captivity.

When Ilona walked into her little town she found her picture in a store window festooned with red, white and blue banners. She was declared a town hero and given special acknowledgement by the townspeople for the way she had so long outwitted the Gestapo. She was treated for lice by the doctor who had been forced to flee and who she was going to forewarn.

And now without papers, identification or money she had to find a way to reestablish contact with her family. Was her mother alive? What about her older sister whom she adored? And what of the Aunt in New York City who had been supplying her with money that enabled her to attend these private schools?

Her school principal got her a train ticket to Paris. She went not knowing where she was headed or what she would find. The principal also made some calls to the Deuxieme Bureau and she got some money from them, then roomed with a friend.

Now with French intelligence she went to their offices in the Eureka Vacuum building. She translated German and Hungarian for them.

A special assignment was given her one day. A Hungarian woman was having a tryst with an American air officer in a Paris hotel. They were sure she was getting classified information from him and passing it on. She kept a diary but it was in Hungarian. Ilona was to become the new chambermaid and read that diary.

The entries proved she was indeed getting information from him and was selling it to the Germans. She was arrested. The officer was sent home.

A more dangerous assignment was given the thirteen year-old girl. Because of her youth she would hardly be suspected of being a courier. The fighting had spread far beyond Paris but eastern France was still occupied. The French wanted to get funds to their members in occupied territory. Ilona was to take the money in her suitcase and ride the train to various towns. There she would meet with various concierges and deliver the money.

Because the Germans had the habit of checking passengers and often their luggage it was decided she should seek out German officers and ride with them. The Gestapo would not check her luggage assuming she was with them.

It worked perfectly as the Germans would tell her of their own little girls like her, lecture her on being careful and in general even handle her suitcase for her.

Later the French admitted for her first several trips they had followed her to be sure she did exactly as told.

When the war ended she married an American officer and moved to the United States.

CHAPTER 9

▼

LXXX
Magda Fontanges

In April of 1931 a beautiful young reporter was sent to Rome to represent some French newspapers. She was Magda Fontanges. She was well recommended with letters from French deputies and Cabinet Ministers as well as various Ambassadors. She stayed only in the very finest hotels and dined at the most fashionable restaurants.

A few months after she arrived she hit the big scoop all reporters dream of. It was an interview with famed Italian dictator, Benito Mussolini.

He was gracious and gave her a lengthy interview which resulted in a front page story. Certainly a welcome addition to her resume. Mussolini went even further— he seduced her as well which seems to have not been all that difficult.

Unofficially Magda soon became the most important woman in Italy. As is too often the case the man becomes bored and seeks new conquests. He saw her less and less and it became evident she was on her way out. In the meantime, however, tongues wagged and the stories flowed of their trysts, probably greatly embellished. But as she faded in Mussolini's eyes she did not in the eyes of Rome. She greatly helped her own cause by handling her own publicity.

Her story was spurred on when she became enraged about too nosy French Ambassador, Count Charles de Chambrum. He was overly interested in her affair with the dictator. She shot him twice but fortunately only slightly wounded him. Once more she was splashed across the front page.

Mussolini thought it funny and laughed.

Her fine? Twenty-five dollars.

But all in all he was tired of her and really blew up when she sold their story to the American Press entitled "I Was Mussolini's Mistress". That did it.

He pushed her off on the Gestapo, sent her to France and there she spied on the French underground in Marseilles and Brussels. From 1940 to 1943 she worked with the Gestapo. She was paid $42.50 per month plus expenses.

There is no record of her after 1943 until 1947 when she came to trial in Paris. Those who knew her in earlier years were shocked to see a haggard old woman with unkempt hair in shabby clothes. This was the woman to whom Mussolini once had said, "One hour of love with you, and Ethiopia means nothing to me".

Her wit was now dulled but she did her best to spice up the trial with stories of intimate visits with Quai d'Orsay ministers. She made one last, desperate bid by hiring famed attorney Dr. Marcel Petiot. It did no good.

As she exited the courtroom after being found guilty she exclaimed, "My only regret is that I wasn't hanged with the Duce, instead of his last mistress, Clara Petacci".

LXXXI
Iva Toguri Aka Tokyo Rose

She became known to thousands of soldiers, sailors and marines across the Pacific in World War II.

Though not engaged in espionage she did excel at another activity that hampered the Allied war effort— propaganda.

Iva Toguri was one of the voices of Tokyo Rose.

She was an American, a second born generation of Japanese and a student of zoological research at the University of California, Los Angeles. She also was interested in drama and speech. Her parents ran a grocery store in Chicago.

In 1941 she received an invitation to visit an uncle in Tokyo. With the threat of war hanging heavy the State Department refused to issue passports to Japan. She went anyway.

After a brief stay she searched for a way to return to America without a passport. And suddenly it was too late—bombs fell on Pearl Harbor. She was trapped in Japan.

The Japanese police arrested her as an enemy alien. Later the charges were dropped and she was released.

But her freedom came with a price. She was to broadcast propaganda against American forces.

Her first program was as 'Ann', short for Orphan Annie. This seemed appropriate in the fact she was indeed orphaned for the war.

She began by speaking softly, seductively to the 'forgotten men, the American fighting men'. Her talk was intermingled with American big band music and folk songs.

The pay was negligible. It started at one hundred yen monthly, about six American dollars. Later it was increased to one hundred forty seven yen.

At her trial she insisted she was forced into this line of work by a man who had become her lover. She did not dare refuse him. Also she stated she had merely read scripts and played music. The continuity was established by Australian Captain Charles Cousins who had been captured at Singapore, and a U.S. army captain she said was named Ince.

Iva felt she would never be caught. Seven other American and Canadian women likewise broadcast for the Japanese. But she was betrayed by the Japanese.

She told the arresting American soldiers she was innocent and had done nothing.

At her trial she first claimed she could not be guilty of treason against the United States as she had married a Portuguese man in 1945 and was now a citizen of that country. Also she had never done anything really harmful to America.

The defense was surprised when recorded tapes were played back with her harsh, cynical laugh following claims that Americans would never get back as all their ships had been sunk.

She was shocked when she was found guilty and sentenced to ten years and a $10,000 fine.

There was no leniency. She served her sentence.

Morale Operations (M.O.)

In addition to the physical tools used by agents there were those especially suited to women's temperament, cunning and skills. These were the rumors put into circulation by Morale Operations designed to cause harm to our enemies. The OSS manual stated, "Rarely can they (rumors) by themselves change basic attitudes. Their function is to confirm suspicions and beliefs already latent; to give sense and direction to fears, resentments or hopes that have been built up by more materialistic causes; to tip the balance when public opinion is in a precarious state." Together with their male counterparts the women learned a good rumor spreads widely in a form close to that of the original story.

The women, using basic stories dreamed up by psychologists and Madison Avenue admen, found it easy to add rumors to those others had as they stood in food lines or waited under hair dryers. In addition they created their own based on current conditions in the country where they were operating. OSS became so sophisticated in it's rumor-mongering that by 1944 they divided them into formal categories. Some examples:

The Confusion Rumor

Fear of inflation is the straightest road to actual inflation. Working on this principle the following were floated:

.The Reichsdrucherei (the German Mint) is printing large amounts of currency.

.The value of the (German) mark in the black markets of Switzerland has dropped considerably.

.Life insurance companies have asked the German government for extensive emergency loans. Because of the large number of deaths in the Reich, these companies are no longer solvent.

The Personal Gossip Attack Rumor

OSS used variations on the theme, "where is Hitler"? OSS would announce through neutral press leaks and its own clandestine publications that Hitler was expected to speak/appear at a certain rally. The announcements were, of course, absolutely false. When Hitler did not appear a subsequent rumor was spread of his death, disappearance, illness, psychotic condition or even flight from Germany. Its purpose was to sow doubt in the minds of the public and armed forces.

The Humorous Rumor

•In mid 1943 the rumor was floated that 'Barbers in Holland are now charging five cents more per shave because German faces are longer these days'. Two months later the rumor was printed in the Providence Journal showing it had not died down.

The Pipe Dream Rumor

•These rumors promised a better life to Axis soldiers who surrendered. Germans in North Africa were told that POWs captured in the Middle East lived pleasant lives and served as chauffeurs for allied Generals. Several captured German airman asked about the assignments and were disappointed to learn the truth.

The Bogeyman Rumor

»In World War 1 a report the German navy was being ordered to make a final suicidal attack against the British caused a navy mutiny. The same rumor was used in WW1I but the war ended before it reached its peak.

The Wedge Driving Rumor

These are insidious and dangerous to use because they exploit religious, racial and other prejudices and will last long after the war ends. Two are taken from OSS files:

•At a dinner recently held in Karin Hall by Goering, beer was served in sacred vessels looted from churches in Northern Italy. To save time and space, Himmler has ordered no distinction be observed in cremations of Protestant and Catholic air-raid victims.

One additional rumor was actually a statement of truth but told in such a way to cause suspicion. In a specific area the story would be spread, "There is absolutely no truth in the statement a certain lake is poisoned". Female agents talking to other women would then discuss a variety of alleged illnesses they, their family or friends were experiencing causing others to examine their own aches or pains. It spread personal concern and worry that their government was not telling them the truth.

Another area that became much more refined and sophisticated during this war was that of disinformation. To protect the truth it was necessary to use a cover of half-truths and outright distortions so the enemy could not tell which was the truth, which manufactured information.

One example of how this could be used came to light after the murder of former Russian NKVD head, Lavrenti Beria. Probably responsible for more deaths than Hitler he was hated and feared with good cause. Whether it was England or America, or possibly even France (or a combination) rumors were slowly leaked over a several year period that he was leaking intelligence to the west. Because such a ploy would be expected it had to be done with the utmost delicacy and secrecy.

Rumors of a fake account set up in Switzerland for him were floated. Money actually was deposited. Eventually he was strangled by his own people in the Kremlin. No positive proof exists it was because of his 'treachery'· Possibly his time was up. We'll never know for sure.

The Proper Dress

Along with the men most of the female agents had to be made as authentic as possible when facing the enemy. It consisted not only of the Germans but in many cases French, Dutch, Polish and Czech citizens who supported and aided the Germans acting as police and informers.

The French Millice were hated even more than the Nazis. Not only did they aid the German cause but they were traitors to their own people. A French agent, or one posing as a Frenchman or woman, might be tripped up by something one of these traitors would recognize that a German might not. Incorrect grammar, an accent that belonged to a different area, lack of a French custom—all could trip up an undercover agent.

A British woman crossing a street might unconsciously look the wrong way for traffic. An American woman could face the wrong way in a theatre walking over seated patrons to her seat. (In Europe they face the people they are walking past rather than the front as is done in America). The way a cigarette was held could be a deadly tip-off. Fillings in teeth or dental bridges had to be changed.

One bureau worked solely with clothing purchased from European refugees. A woman's underwear of European manufacture was as essential as her outer clothing. Where it was necessary to sew a seam it had to be with the right gauge and type of thread as well as the proper stitching. Buttons had to be sewn on by thread-ing the holes in parallel instead of criss-cross fashion. Inside pockets were fitted on each side and if the suit happened to be tailored to order, a tailors slip would be on the inside left pockets of the jacket. Normally plain bone buttons were used but suspender buttons were sometimes marked "elegant" or "mode de Paris", as was found to be customary on both German and French clothes. For the clothing shop OSS supplied a tailor while Polish Intelligence furnished a cobbler.

Accessories were varied in origin. Shoelaces were German, handkerchiefs were British imitations and towels were made in Ireland. Since the stock of genuine articles was insufficient, a Camouflage Section was established in August 1944 to manufacture additional accessories as well as lead pencils to be used as conceal-ment devices, belt buckles for the same purpose, letter drops and the like. Women's undergarments offered special hiding places. Cover stories were carefully man-ufactured. An agent would almost always be asked the color of streetcars in a town he or she claimed to be from. A time period could be important as in some cities the colors did change.

Addresses of bombed out streets were essential so the agent could show one of them as his former address knowing it could not be verified. The same with an office the agent might be using as cover for a past job.

Names of the City officials had to be dredged and committed to memory.

Radio operators were taken to remote areas to practice sending and receiving messages. Instructors kept all the sheets of paper used by students in their cipher work because it was found that operators had a tendency to repeat the same mistakes, especially in the field working under stress. Badly garbled cables could often be decoded by the instructors who were familiar with each agent's typical mistakes.

In addition the 'fist' of an operator could be so well known to the base receiver that someone else sending under his/her name would be recognized as an interloper.

Papers and money had to be properly aged. This was done by rubbing them in ashes or in a powder made of crushed rock and by rounding the corners with sandpaper. Alternately, training officers carried documents in their hip and shirt pockets until they were suitably sweated.

In many cases OSS office floors were covered with foreign currency which was walked over for days to destroy its new appearance. One woman reported a newly designed identity card the Germans had just dreamed up. It bore a nine-digit number and confused headquarters. Soon it was deciphered. Each prefectural city in France had a number which was represented by the first three digits. Five other digits gave the date, month and year of the bearer's birth. The last one, odd or even, showed whether the person was male or female. A British agent obtained a complete list of all the cities in France and their corresponding numbers.

Toys of the OSS and CIA

Special secret gadgetry has fascinated the public whose awareness of it has been heightened by the James Bond movies.

The author of the James Bond stories was Ian Fleming who, as a British intelligence agent in World War II, was also an instructor at the highly secret Camp X in Canada. Through this camp many OSS and British agents trained for their work against the Axis powers. But development of these items mostly has come from the Research and Development laboratories who listen to the needs of agents in the field.

Famed Dr. Stanley Lovell, who headed the OSS research laboratories, came up with some of the more exotic 'toys' used in that war. Some of his items included...

'The Firefly', a device designed to blow up tanks and motor vehicles when dropped in a gas tank. It took awhile to activate taking the doomed vehicle some distance from where it was sabotaged.

'The Hedy'. whose purpose was to create panic and turmoil giving the agent time to escape if in peril. Including gallic acid, a pallet of black powder and potassium chlorate it released volumes of gases which escaped through a narrow opening giving a terrifying whistling sound followed by a puff of black powder when activated. In the mass confusion that followed the agent could disappear.

'The Dog Drag', a canvas bag containing an ampoule of strong smelling chemicals that would permeate its sack when crushed. It was then to be dragged behind a fleeing agent to destroy his/her scent if being pursued by soldiers with scent seeking dogs.

'Pneumonia' was a poison causing immediate death and leaving no trace in case of autopsy. The agent was botulism toxin. In its gelatin capsule it was the size of a pinhead. It was principally designed for Chinese prostitutes to slip into the food or drink of Japanese clients. The agents receiving these deadly items, and noting their size, wondered about the mental health of the OSS labs. Deciding to test it on a donkey they found it had no effect and shelved them. Had they told Washington what they had done they would have been told the donkey has a total natural immunity to the deadly effects of botulism.

'The L Pill', a rubber coated cyanide pill designed for the suicide of an agent should he/she prefer that to capture and the inevitable torture.

'The K Pill', a knockout drop not unlike what we used to call a Mickey Finn. Dropped in an enemy's drink he quickly became groggy, then unconscious giving the agent time to disappear.

'The E&E Suppository MK 1' kit. A complete escape tool kit housed in a rubber capsule that can be carried in the anus. It contains a saw, file and knife blades as well as a drill and set of reamers. It is held in place by the sphincter muscle.

'Little Joe', a hand-held crossbar weapon that used a powerful rubber band to propel a wooden dart fitted with a metal point. It was a silent weapon designed to dispose of a sentry.

A variety of cigarettes, pipes, eye-glasses, ladies combs, lipsticks, compacts and cigarette lighters were fitted to fire a .22 caliber bullet.

The 'pocket incendiary Ml' was a flat black celluloid case filled with a petroleum jelly fuel. Time delay devices similar to a pencil allowed the agent to be some distance away when it took off. When ignited it burned with an intense ferocity and caused many fires.

The 'anerometer' was an explosive weapon designed to be concealed in an enemy aircraft and explode at a certain altitude. Its explosive effect was greater than a direct hit by a 75 mm. shell.

Since the end of WWII strides in electronics and chips have made gadget/weapons even more exotic. Transmitters of the 007 genre utilized cocktail olives that were actually transmitters. The swizzle stick became the antenna. Or, if a non-drinker the transmitter could be put in a sugar cube.

Ten years after WWII the OSO (Office of Special Operations) devised a miniature bomb that could be fastened to a wall or any other item by a wad of chewing gum. It could be exploded by a car radio signal some distance away.

President Nasser of Egypt built a large radio tower in 1954. The CIA secretly placed a bomb in the basement that could be detonated by a transmitter some miles away. In 1956 Alien Dulles ordered the bomb to be exploded. Nothing happened. Someone had obviously found and removed the bomb.

Agents can easily televise special operations. The lens of the camera is about the size of a pea and easily concealed as a tie-tac, in a hat or a woman's piece of jewelry.

Many of the television shows that produce pictures taken by a secret camera are using this device. Today's cost of the item, $3,600.

A chemically treated handkerchief will pick up traces of factory fumes and identify the source.

An innocent desk sponge used for moistening stamps and envelopes will capture the body chemistry and is accurate enough to reveal who had been in the room.

Chemicals that are undetectable will induce problems from mild headaches to hallucinations. In addition chemicals exist to increase the sex drive. This enables Ravens and Swallows to spend less time setting their pigeons up.

Using microchips has unleashed a whole new field for fertile minds to play in. One agency attached a radio transmitter to the back of a housefly. A not too practical use to be sure.

But the term "pigeon drop" had a new meaning when the C1A used pigeons equipped with microchip transmitters. By use of a laser beam they would be guided to the ledge or windowsill of a particular bedroom. Once there the trained pigeon would peck at a button that released the transmitter, then fly back home.

It is possible to eavesdrop on the conversation in a room by measuring the vibrations off of the glass from outside.

In 1969 a clever plan bugged the left shoe of a U.S. Diplomat in Bucharest. His 'maid' had taken his shoes to a cobbler for some repairs. He inserted a tiny transmitter into the left heel. It was powered by five mercury cells. Two small holes were drilled in the front of the heel and this controlled the on-off switch. In the morning the 'maid' would insert a pin in one hole to start it. At night the other hole would be used to disengage it.

Body sculptors were at work in fashioning a fake nipple molded into flesh colored rubber. It was powered by body heat.

A radio tooth could be equipped with the transmitter as well as aerial, batteries and sensors.

The KGB devised a way to use a still camera to pick up sexual activity. A wire attached to the bedsprings would run to the camera. The weight of a single person would not trigger it but two people would activate it.

Always seeking one-upmanship (and not wanting to ruin a good time) some agents insisted on sex on the floor or in the bathtub. To handle this problem Swallows were given vaginal transmitters that turned on during intercourse. The transmitters then started the cameras.

Many of these highly specialized gadgets are available to the public and advertised in catalogues.

The "telephone watchman" can easily be attached to any phone. You can detect an intruder anywhere in the world.

For $50 or less you can now obtain the "tap detector" which flashes a red light to alert you to an outside tap or even if someone lifts an extension phone.

An item about the size of a matchbox, the MCS 1101, will transmit conversation between the agent and his mark up to a quarter of a mile away. Cost: about $1,000.

Add to these a variety of items such as telephone taps, room bugs, an FM telephone transmitter kit the size of a dime, a 'pen microphone', 'voice activated recorders that go up to 10 hours', 'spy paper that dissolves in water', 'scramblers for phones', 'tape and bug detectors', 'body wire detector', 'fax scramblers', and 'magnascanners to detect hidden weapons' and we have entered the world of highly sophisticated weaponry never dreamed of in the hectic days of WWII.

Post World War II

Possibly based on the recent affirmative action going on in America, but more probably likely due to their performance, the CIA has allotted 40% of its hiring slots to women. These women will be hired at all levels of the agency, not just record keeping.

Operations and performance of women during WWII gave more insight than we had ever had before. The proof of their performance could be measured in a way that cannot be disputed or explained away.

But a more sinister side to America became more prevalent than it had ever been before in our history...that of betrayal.

Not that either sex had a corner on it but for various reasons more Americans than ever seemed to be committing treason against their own country, men and women.

Idealism played a big part in it. Communist spies had somehow bought the big lie and were into feeling their cause greater than any law since it was for the 'common people'.

Patriotism played a major role in many peoples lives and there were, of course, those whose services were for sale to the highest bidder. They will always be around.

Then there were those who spied under duress or blackmail. There was the fear of being exposed as a homosexual or possibly those with relatives under control of a foreign government. In a study of intelligence agents and their causes. Professor Sidney Hook, of New York University, has analyzed the motive.

He declared, "Ideologically motivated espionage agents cost much less than others. But of far greater importance is the fact that they are more reliable and more willing to undertake greater risks. Tasks that are too hazardous for the professional spy are eagerly assumed by the political spy".

At the same the Professor warned of a mixture of mis-guided messianic zeal and misguided idealism which, in his belief, produced such spies as atom spy Harry Gold, Klaus Fuchs and others.

It was the belief of Rebecca West in her, 'Meaning of Treason', "the psychotic will very readily take sides against his own country. He is as if commanded by heaven to be a prop for any neighboring power which desire to swallow his fatherland. He hates the people around him, he hates his fellow countrymen, because he hates the real world".

America, too, had to look to its own slipping morals and ethics after the war. The lure of communism and materialism found fertile ground in many who no longer realized society lived by a code of ethics and morality. The excess of the lost generation of the 1960s was all too evident.

Psychiatrists around the world state that some trai-tors belong to a class of those known as 'psychopathic'. In further explaining that conclusion they go on to state that the term does mean he or she is insane but rather suffers from an open instability of thought, feeling and behavior. The fact so many spies work for both sides, friend and enemy, seems to be make it credible. Heredity also plays a part. Atom spy, Dr. Klaus Fuchs, had one sister who committed suicide, another that was close to a breakdown.

Money, like the woman's use of sex, is not always a determining factor. Under orders from their governments both Nazi and Communist spies have worked for nothing. Gerhart Eisler, the #1 Soviet spy in America, lived in abject poverty in New York. Magda Fontanges was once the mistress of Mussolini and later served as a Gestapo agent. She was paid the magnificent sum of $42.50 a month during her term of service. The perfect motive for agents may have been caught by Dr. C.G. Jung who said it was, "the senseless emptiness of their lives". Germany's master spy of the First World War, Von Rintelen, organized strikes in England and blew up factories. He died in England, never returning to his fatherland because he had always hated the Prussians. In fact he would not even accept their money.

As long as people hate and distrust one another there will always be the need for spying. And while it can often prove another nation's intentions are not honorable it can sometimes put to rest unfounded rumors that bring tensions to the surface. Women are in the field of intelligence to stay. They are charming, sometimes beautiful, clever, cunning and—dangerous.

LXXIX
Elisabeth Dorhofer

In July 1950 the Soviets penetrated Weimar, in the Soviet zone of Germany. They employed a German,

Hans Kurt Pape, at first, then assigned a 'Captain Burda' to work with him. Their target was to learn the identity of Germans who were working for American intelligence.

Pape went to Frankfurt and opened a studio which ostensibly was to help young pretty women become movie stars by providing photographic portfolios which he took.

Together with Burda they discovered a young, beautiful Czech woman named Elisabeth Dorhofer. With her body and her warm smile and outstanding personality they felt she would make an excellent spy. She agreed.

Burda took her to Czechoslovakia where she trained for long hours in espionage followed by extensive love making at night. Going back to Frankfurt after her training she frequented bars where American servicemen visited. Her novel way of getting their attention was by giving out nude photos of herself. When she felt she had a close relationship she made offers of up to 10,000 marks for information on U.S. Army operations.

A U.S. army officer reported her actions. In addition Pape made a decision to add to his income by becoming a double agent. He offered his services to the CIA.

Dorhofer was placed under surveillance and finally was picked up at the Czech border as she made one of her frequent crossings. She had with her at the time documents and photographs and the canister of a gas mask the Soviets wanted to duplicate. Tried before an American court, she was given a seven year sentence.

LXXXIII
Jeanne Macleod Aka Banda

The death of Mata Hari, certainly the best-known
female spy in history, did not in any way inhibit the
service of future women who sought to spy for a variety of reasons.

Mata left a daughter, Jeanne Louise MacLeod, who
went to live with relatives in Batavia, the capital of Java,
after the loss of her mother. She took the name of Banda.

It would be hard to imagine her Dutch heritage when
she appeared with her black hair and almond eyes. She
also had a good figure, one sufficient to turn heads.

A few months later Banda left her relatives home to
be with a Dutch official who was 40 years her senior.
Soon they were married. The marriage turned out most
beneficial to Banda who found everything in her husband a woman could want. As a father figure, lover,
counselor and friend he brought out the best in her.

A short time later he died leaving her quite well off.
With this largesse she threw parties for the elite and soon
became the darling of Batavian society.

In 1942 her life changed considerably when the
Japanese invaded Indonesia and she was visited by a
Japanese officer. Demanding her cooperation he threatened to expose her as the daughter of Mata Hari. She
complied. They allowed her to continue with her lavish
parties but with the proviso they would select the guests.
The fates that spun around her famous mother began
surrounding Banda.

At one of her parties she was introduced to a leader of
one of the clandestine parties seeking freedom. She fell

in love with his ideas—and then him. He was destined to become one of the most important figures in the struggle for freedom.

It followed that she joined his movement and soon became one of the most important figures in espionage against the Japanese. Banda got a hold of the battle plans for Guadalcanal including air and naval information vital to the American military. Before the war was to end her reports had reached the main intelligence headquarters of Allied intelligence.

With the end of the war she switched her talents to helping the freedom movement against the Dutch. She became involved with a Dutch official and solicited information from him to help her Indonesian lover.

With the final independence of Indonesia Banda visited America lecturing on behalf of the new country. Her plans were to once more live in Batavia and continue her lavish lifestyle.

Fate stepped in in the form of American Intelligence. Lacking critical intelligence in China they desperately sought someone to infiltrate that country's bamboo curtain. Though she had no reason to help America, she agreed.

In China she spent many days in the camp of Mao Tse-tung, leader of the Communist forces. Her report, though proved accurate, was not pleasing to America. There was no hope of Chiang Kai-shek's forces defeating Mao.

Apparently now loving the intrigue that ensnared her mother Banda accepted a new assignment from America—Korea. Fearing unknown factors in North

Korea they awaited her reports. Once more they were unfavorable but accurate.

She reported a Communist attack, backed by Russia, was planned against the south. As too often happens the report was not heeded.

After the attack was launched fate dealt a final, fatal blow to Banda. During the time she worked with the Indonesians against the Dutch one of her informers was a young Communist. His name was Mato.

In 1950 as she walked down a dusty street in North Korea she ran into Mato, now a Communist commissar.

He accused her of being an American spy and ordered her immediate arrest.

Without a trial she was proclaimed guilty and executed at 5:45 a.m., thirty three years later to the minute of her mother, Mata Hari.

LXXXIV
Lydia Kuzazov and the KGB Sex School

There are many reasons why women will use their bodies in the pursuit of intelligence. They are:

1. Love
2. Patriotism
3» Money or social gain
4. Revenge
5» Coercion or blackmail

While the Soviets appealed to #2, Patriotism, it was normally #5, coercion or blackmail that brought them their desired results. Many governments have used bugged rooms to photograph or taped sexual encounters for blackmail later but only one has established an official school to train its men and women.

Russia, under the tutelage of Laventia Beria, began its school in late 1945. Beria had always felt sex was one of the strongest weapons in the subverting of other nationals and gathering of intelligence.

He himself was well into sexual perversions as he dallied with young girls in sodomy and oral sex.

He solidified his own position in what became the KGB by setting up his immediate superior in a compromising situation requiring him to resign. Beria promptly stepped into his shoes and established the school.

The KGB was broken into four sections or directorates: To show the importance attached to sex the first two were assigned to sexual activities.

#1 deals with foreign operations including covert operations, espionage and assassinations. One of its subunits is known as SMERSH which handles assassination of defectors or anyone who the KGB feels has betrayed it. It also deals in fake paper including, but not limited to, codes, passes, fake passports, cover stories and even counterfeiting.

#2 handles the recruiting of Swallows (female) and Ravens (male) operatives.

The mostly young men and women taken into the school have no idea of what they will be expected to do for their government. Like the U.S. Marines who totally tear down their recruits, then rebuild them in the Marine mold, the Soviets likewise first destroy their students inhibitions.

First they are lectured on the importance of loyalty to the Fatherland and that sex in carrying out those duties is right, proper and expected. Not only sex but additional duties that may well include poisons administered in food and drink.

Candidates are selected on the basis of attractiveness and ability to communicate well. In the case of male homosexuals many are given the choice of their new jobs or prison.

They are given a heavy dose of propaganda in a school in Moscow. Here they are put in typically American scenes such as stores, restaurants and even schools. They wear American clothes, use American expressions including slang, learn how to board buses, buy theater tickets, how to tip, how to blend in. Their English is carefully monitored to eliminate traces of accent where needed.

After their indoctrination in ideology and party loyalty they begin their training at the Verkhonoye House of Love outside Leningrad. It is headed by Lydia Kuzazov, a KGB Colonel, who was a former Swallow and thoroughly versed in sexual delights.

Svetlana, a 16 year old girl is thought to be a good candidate. Her father is an electrical engineer and a loyal party member. Her mother works for the railroads. They are delighted when their daughter tells them she has been approached by a party member who wants her to go to work for the government. She will be given a small salary and her own apartment, almost unheard of. When she is finally taken to the school her parents were delighted. After three weeks of indoctrination she was transferred to Verkhonoye for an eye opening first day.

Together with about 25 other men and women who averaged about 20 years of age she was lectured by an official who told them they were to be open and not bothered by what they would now see. They sat down to see a film that was pure pornographic. Every possible angle of sexual intercourse including oral and anal was shown. Svetlana, a virgin, was shocked beyond belief. She was further dismayed when a woman had each of the candidates remove their clothing and walk around naked to remove any inhibitions. Following that they were given large quantities of alcohol and told anything they could do for the Fatherland, they must do. It was the patriotic thing to do. The following day the tempo increased. A couple proceeded to the front of the room where a large mat lay. They removed their clothing and began making love while the instructors advised their recruits to observe carefully just how the woman stimulated the man.

The next step involved one on one situations. Some cadets were brought in and the women instructed to seduce them. Their actions, including speech, were monitored carefully. The cadets were to resist to a point. When they finally gave in they were taken to the women's rooms where the assignation was completed. The male recruits suffered severe indignities. All were handsome, few homosexual. Yet they were forced to do anything their partners wanted including making love to homely women. One of the Ravens said later that during his stay at the school several of the men committed suicide.

Svetlana later defected and gave graphic details of her schooling and activities which finally became too much to bear. The practice of defecting bears terrifying consequences. One Swallow who did so was attacked in Berlin while taking a walk. She was knocked unconscious and thrown in the path of a speeding car. She died without regaining consciousness.

Another, Maria Moralaes, was the widow of a Marxist leader in the Dominican Republic. Disenchanted with Communism she went to work as a double agent for the CIA. Recalled to Moscow she quickly disappeared. In late December 1971 the police found a suitcase containing her legs. Three days later a second suitcase turned up with her arms and torso.

Russia's Swallow and Ravens created many major problems for those who opposed Communism. Sex and blackmail were great weapons the Russians proved time and again.

One turned swallow who had gone through her special training at one of the Soviet schools said about 6,000 people were trained annually in these schools. They were so diversified that the Chinese, Japanese, Korean, Indonesians, Filipino and Burmese had their own "School of the Peoples of the East" in Moscow. In addition another existed in Vladivostok and a new one was being established in Manchuria.

All were handpicked and their training included marksmanship, codes, how to start armed uprisings, organization of strikes and civil and guerrilla warfare.

An unexpected and humorous reaction to one blackmail attempt came when President Sukarno of Indonesia was taken into a private room at the Kremlin. Some requests were made for special treatment of Communists within his country.

When he refused they dimmed the lights and showed him one of their sex tapes showing him engaging in sex acts with a swallow. When it was over they sat back to await his reaction but they were shocked.

He thought they were wonderful and asked if he could have a copy to take back home to show his people their leader in action.

Further exploration of agents, incidents and provocations and the manner in which Russia utilizes them will become even more evident as we examine specific cases.

LXXXV
Shi Pei Pu

One of the most intriguing stories of espionage occurred in China in 1964. It involved a French diplomat, Bernard Bouriscot, and a beautiful Chinese singer and dancer. Her name was Shi Pei Pu. She intrigued Bouriscot with her talents and also the fact she spoke flawless French.

They held their liaisons in Peking where Bouriscot was totally unaware she was an ardent Communist, known even to Chairman Mao. In the intervening months Bouriscot was transferred to Saudi Arabia and left Shi Pei behind.

He was surprised to receive notice that he was the father of a son born to Shi Pei. He frantically began trying to arrange his transfer back to Peking.

When it was completed he ran into a snag. The Cultural Revolution was in full sway and the opera disbanded. The Red Guard was everywhere.

Eventually he tracked her down only to be caught with her by the Red Guard. Blackmail followed.

If he didn't agree to send them sensitive documents going into and out of the French Embassy, Shi Pei would be sent to an agricultural camp.

Though transferred back to Paris, Bouriscot continued sending what he could. Then he arranged for a cultural exchange which brought Shi Pei to Paris. She moved in with him immediately.

Their love nest was interrupted when both were arrested by the French counterintelligence who had them both under surveillance.

The truly bizarre aspect of the whole affair was an examination of Shi Pei revealed he was a fully developed male. The child, supposedly fathered by Bouriscot, was actually purchased in a marketplace in Peking.

In attempting to explain the embarrassing situation Bouriscot said they had had sexual relations in the dark. It was his opinion, he insisted, that the child was actually a product of their love. He further insisted he had spied out of love and his act was not treasonable.

Shaking his head in disbelief that a man could have sexual relations with another man and not know it, the judge sentenced Bouriscot to six years in prison.

Their story was retold in 1988 in a very successful Broadway play, M. Butterfly.

CHAPTER 10

▼

LXXXVI
Sylvia Rafael Aka Patricia Rox

Very little is known of Israel's intelligence operatives. Their operations are understandably most secretive.

Its formal name is "The Institution for Intelligence and Special Assignments." It is given full freedom by the public who admire and believe in its eye-for-an-eye tradition. It is actually a descendant of a group of intelligence and security forces that date back to pre-independence days.

Under the Mossad all avenues of intelligence gathering, covert operations, kidnapping and assassinations are carried out.

The Israeli use both male and female operatives. One of their best women is Sylvia Rafael.

In 1973 Sylvia was sent into Norway as a member of a Mossad hit team. Their mission was to avenge the killing if 11 Israeli athletes at Munich. Head of the responsible Black September gang was Alt Hassan Salameh. In addition to being known as the one who organized the

Munich massacre he also was believed responsible for other murders and the hijacking of airplanes.

The team waited its chance and finally struck in Oslo. They were pleased the man had been efficiently and quietly dispatched.

To their chagrin they learned they had killed the wrong man. The one they had shot was actually a Moroccan waiter.

A dispute still lingers over whether or not Norweigan police actually helped part of the Israeli hit-team depart. What is known is two were detained with Canadian passports. They were listed as Leslie and Patricia Roxburger. Among their paperwork was a phone number of Oslo's Mossad chief.

A deeper check revealed the two were actually Sylvia Rafael and Abraham Gehmer.

They were tried and received an extremely light sentence of five and a half years.

Sylvia was released after serving less than two years and returned to Israel where she no doubt still serves the Mossad.

Mossad's central office is on Oliphant Street in the Talbieh section of Jerusalem.

LXXXVII
Rima Tannous—Therese Halsa

While Arab women are held in check more by the men they still are useful in many ways. Terrorism is one field they can and do serve well in.

Today it is estimated over half of the leaders of terrorist organizations are women. They can more easily infiltrate certain areas and institutions. Their flowing garments give them great areas of concealment for bombs and weapons.

One of the more infamous terrorist groups was known as Black September. Two of its top agents were women.

Rima Tannous and Therese Halsa received their training in one of the camps dedicated to young terrorists. One of their missions involved the hijacking of a Sabena flight from Brussels to Tel Aviv.

Two men joined them in Brussels where the four partied for three days prior to the flight. They fully enjoyed their time and spent it eating, drinking and engaging in sex with one another.

The day of the hijacking came. Both of the women carried a heavy cardboard box of explosives containing a hand grenade that could be activated with a pull of the ring. In addition the women wore girdles made of explosive fabric. And finally they carried detonators in their brassieres.

The plane was taken over in mid-flight and forced to land at Lod Airport. Here the Israeli paratroopers took over. They stormed the plane and killed the two men. The women were not killed and later answered questions.

Rima claimed to have been orphaned as a child and taken to a convent until she reached her seventeenth birthday when she became a nurse. During that period she was raped by an aide, then had an affair with a doctor who hooked her on drugs. Next she was introduced to the Arab guerrillas.

As is often the case with the Israelis no further records exist to show punishment or the future of these two women. They could well be working for the Mossad now.

LXXXVIII
Judith Coplon

A person who turns on his or her country for whatever reason is always an anathema to loyal and patriotic citizens. One such person was Judith Coplon, the first American civilian to be tried and convicted of treason against her native land.

Her childhood was one of respect and honor as she grew up within the strict discipline of her Jewish home. She exhibited a love for music and the arts.

She attended Barnard College and graduated with honors in 1943. During this period her inquisitive mind had switched to politics and eventually liberal idealism. She became fascinated with the teachings of Lenin and Marx as well as the Russian revolution. Communist philosophy soon captured her mind.

Following graduation she accepted employment as a journalist in the Economic Welfare Section of the Justice Department in New York City.

Two years later she moved to Washington with the Foreign Agents Registration Division where she became a political analyst. She reviewed classified information and reports dealing with foreign officials. Because her office worked closely with the FBI she also saw reports from the FBI detailing those they felt were a possible threat to national security. She had access to all such files.

In 1948 her superior work was acknowledged by U.S. Attorney General, Tom Clark.

Another evaluation of her work, however, was not so pleasant. Her fellow workers reported her slanting of reports to favor the Soviet Union and other Communist countries. This tallied with reports the FBI had of leaks of information which were traced to her department. She was put under surveillance.

They watched her as she began leaving weekends stating she was going to visit her parents in Brooklyn. In early January two FBI agents followed her to Manhattan where she casually strolled down the street, obviously waiting for someone. A well-dressed man passed her and entered a nearby restaurant. She followed and joined him for dinner. When they left they went to the subway going in different directions. A short distance later the man, using evasive tactics, waited until the subway doors were closing before squeezing out thus getting rid of the agent tailing him.

It was felt, however, he had to be a Soviet agent and the FBI posted a man outside the Soviet consulate-general the next morning. Several hours later their man emerged and went to his apartment. When asked about his tenant the manager stated he was Valentin Gubitchev who was an employee of the United Nations. Gubitchev was listed as a construction engineer and an international civil servant which did not give him diplomatic immunity.

Several weekends later her trips took a sudden turn. She drove off in a car with a young man. They drove to a hotel in Baltimore and registered as Mr. and Mrs. H. Shapiro of Hartford, Connecticut.

The FBI moved into action with recorders, microphones and even X-ray machines designed to take silhouette pictures through walls. Taking the room next to the couple they sat through hours of talk and sex. No politics were discussed. The following night the previous evenings activities were simply repeated and nothing gained to further the FBI's case against her. There was little doubt she was transferring sensitive information to the Russians.

The FBI created a false letter stating three Soviet members of AMTORG (Russian Trade Organization in America) were actually FBI agents. The letter was put on Coplon's desk in February 1948. She immediately asked to leave early on Friday to spend time with her parents.

As the agents tailed her she got off the train and took the subway to Manhattan once more. Coming down the street on the opposite side was Gubitchev. She crossed over and, as she passed him, switched her purse to her left arm. As they came together they talked briefly. She was seen opening her handbag but they could not see Gubitchev take anything from it. Because they had no solid evidence the FBI called it off.

On March 3 the FBI made one more attempt to catch her. Through a tap on her phone they learned she was once more going to New York. This time she was provided with an official looking letter stating, falsely, that AMTORG's American legal representative was working for the FBI.

This time a small FBI army awaited the rendezvous. Twenty agents and seven radio-equipped cars were on hand. Five were assigned to Glubitchev, two were stationed inside the Italian restaurant where Coplon first met him, five were inside Penn station and teams of two were at the 191st and 193rd subway stations.

Aware they were being tailed the couple walked alone for some time ignoring each other. Then they boarded the subway and once more barely squeezed out the subway doors as they closed to lose the man inside. Several hours later they were found again in a a lonely section of the Greenwich Village. This time they were accosted and told, "I am an agent of the FBI. You are both under arrest".

At FBI headquarters they were strip-searched. Coplon was found to have the false letter planted by the FBI and thirty-four top secret documents. She was outraged. Their meetings, she stated, were simply those of a couple in love.

As the sensational trial got underway she based her innocence on the fact she and Gubitchev were simply lovers and the documents she had were to be used as background for a novel she was writing. The newspapers played it up as the problem of two lovers and the public fell partly in line.

The prosecution pushed her into a corner stating again and again that it was all for true love and that Gubitchev was going to divorce his wife and marry her.

Then the bomb shell came when the prosecution said if she was truly in love with only him why did she register two nights in a hotel with a Mr. H. Shapiro.

Losing her composure on the stand she screamed at her attorney, "You son-of-a-bitch, 1 told you this would happen. How could you let it happen with my mother in the courtroom."

The love angle now destroyed she turned to the secret documents she claimed were to be used only to write her novel.

The jury did not buy it and after twenty seven hours of deliberation found her guilty as well as Gubitchev who could not claim diplomatic immunity.

She was sentenced to forty months to ten years in prison. In the second trial for Gubitchev both received additional sentences of fifteen years.

Through a technicality Coplon was released by a Court of Appeal. They pointed out she had been arrested without a warrant and in addition wire tapping had gone on even though none of that evidence was ever used.

In a hoped for bargain for exchange of prisoners with Russia Gubitchev was deported. None of the American captives to be released were, showing Russian treachery.

So the justice system Judith Coplon had turned her back on and tried to destroy wound up freeing her. She served little time for her crime.

LXXXIX
Marion Miller

For many women their service lay not in facing a snarling foreign enemy but rather danger within their own community in America.

The scene was set during the turbulent 1950s in Los Angeles when a young mother, Marion Miller, received a letter that changed her life.

The year was 1950 and she had a brand new baby as well as a two year old. Her husband, Paul, was a poster artist with his own sign shop in their garage. Marion gave piano lessons to augment their income.

The letter invited her to attend an organizational conference of the Los Angeles Committee for Protection of

Foreign Born. The letter was full of references to the 'police state' mentality of America and that fascists using Gestapo methods had control of the Justice Department.

It was so far to the left that her husband insisted she mail it to the FBI since it must be a Communist front.

Just a week later as she was feeding her baby an FBI agent appeared to talk with her. He said the FBI likewise felt this organization had to be a front but that the government had insufficient evidence to label them as subversive.

"Would you go to that meeting and report to the Bureau what happens?" he asked.

Though she had enough to do with two small children she felt it was little enough she could do for her country. She agreed.

She sat among 75 people at that first meeting. She was totally shocked at the hatred and anti-American tone as speaker after speaker excoriated America accusing it of germ warfare in Korea, plans to control the world for Wall Street and anything else they could dream up.

She sat at her typewriter late into the night typing up a full report of what was said and the names she had been able to retain. After mailing it in she felt satisfied that she had done her duty and went back to being a wife and mother.

But it was just the beginning as the FBI liked her report so much they had another request. Would she join the Committee to keep track of its members?

With her husband they explored all aspects of the proposal. They would both appear to be embracing everything they disagreed with and found reprehensible.

They knew their neighbors would turn against them and they would lose old friends. But on the other hand it would be a service to America.

She slept uneasily through the night.

The next morning's newspaper contained the latest casualty figures from Korea. She wondered how many mothers would learn of their sons' death this day. It convinced her.

In November 1950 she joined the Los Angeles Committee for Protection of Foreign Born. In its tawdry room near skid row in Los Angeles she spent hours doing clerical work. Within 60 days she was invited to join the Communist Party. She was then informed they would not tolerate a split family and forced her husband, Paul, to also join.

Their time and their home were totally absorbed by the Party. There were numerous assignments to study, picket, raise funds and do some propaganda campaigns. Party members entered their home without even knocking and held meetings. Their revolutionary talk alienated their neighbors who turned their backs on them.

She recalled her new comrades' were strange and neurotic people. They lived in a dream world where everyone was plotting against them and the Soviet Union. Their claims to love mankind were belied by their inability to trust anyone. On top of that she was offended by the fact they were completely without humor.

In an understandable desire to shield her babies from this type of thinking she saw they attended Sunday School at their Temple and personally taught them to be respectful and considerate and to love and appreciate their parents and grandparents.

She was giving piano lessons to her son, Paul Jr., who was quite talented. But the Party work interfered constantly to his bewilderment. Finally he quit.

But more problematic than that was that he had now reached the age for membership in Communist youth groups. They began putting pressure on Marion to send him. She invented numerous colds, sore throats and other medical problems to keep him from joining.

One night at dinner a Communist functionary named Fanya simply walked into their home shortly after they had eaten dinner.

"I'd like to talk with your son", she demanded. There was no request or courtesy shown.

As her son faced this mannish woman she first asked if he went to Sunday School. When he answered in the affirmative she gave an accusative look to Marion then asked him, "And what do you think about the Chinese People's Republic?"

When the boy looked bewildered she blurted, "You don't know about the heroic Chinese people and their struggle against the fascist warmongers"?

He replied he did not.

She launched into a tirade, then asked him about his feelings towards police, picket lines, trade unions. Wall Street and the atomic bomb.

After she dismissed him she told his mother, "You've made grave mistakes. Comrade. You must educate your children to their Marxist responsibilities."

After she stormed out Marion reevaluated herself as a mother and patriot. There was no doubt her children were suffering as other children came less and less to play. The neighbors were turning their backs on her. How far could she let this go without bringing permanent harm to her children?

She brought her concerns to the FBI who were sympathetic. They told her she could quit at any time but her work was most important. Could she hold on just a little longer?

But the work was taking its toll on her body. In March 1955 she went to the doctor with severe stomach pains. She was told she was under emotional tension and had stomach ulcers. She had to have extended bed rest with peace and quiet.

The FBI immediately told her to take a leave of absence. Even the Communists had to agree.

On the last day of her convalescence two attorneys from the Department of Justice called to tell her they now had enough evidence to prove the Committee was indeed a Communist front. She gave a sigh of relief. It was over.

On October 3, 1955, she went to Washington, D.C. and spent five days on the witness stand telling all she knew. The examiner found her testimony compelling and the Committee was declared a front and must register with the Attorney General as such. She headed home, thrilled it was all behind her.

But the dirty work had just begun. When she reached Los Angeles she saw a troubled look on her husband's face. He showed her a mimeographed sheet entitled, "An Open Letter". In it she was attacked as one who hated the foreign born, had stolen records from the party and other lies typical of Communist smear tactics. It had been sent to every home on their street.

That night her son asked if she was a spy. Then the threatening phone calls came calling her a Judas and other vile names. A rock came through the window telling them they had better sell their home immediately, "or else". Even the few children that had still come to play with her children disappeared.

The next day Paul went to the FBI and police who had promised protection but how? Could they make other children come to play as before?

Finally they went to the press and the full story was printed together with pictures. The calls came once more but this time they were warm and friendly.

Paul Jr's teacher read the news article to the entire class. The truth had surfaced. She knew the ordeal was over when her son came in one night and asked if he might start taking piano again.

A phone call came to her husband one night from a man saying he was Ronald Reagan.

"Sure, and I'm the Shah of Iran," her husband replied.

But it was really Reagan, then with General Electric. He had read the story and wanted to talk with them.

Shortly after that they had dinner with Ronald and Nancy in their Palisades home and a film was discussed.

I first met Marion in early 1996 when, as program Chairman for the Laguna Hills Kiwanis Club, she introduced me as their speaker. I had no idea of her background and she didn't volunteer it.

After another member had alerted me to her special background I persuaded her to give me a Readers Digest reprint of her unusual story.

I am proud to include her as one of the special ladies who risked a lot in service to her nation.

XC
Haydee Tamara Bunke Aka Laura Martinez

The Russians, always suspicious of any activity by the west, were also spying on their communist partners. The paranoid Kremlin saw intrigue everywhere, even in other communist nations.

Haydee Tamara Bunke was the daughter of a German Communist professor of languages in Argentina. She was extremely loyal to the communist party having been so taught by her father.

Changing her name to Laura Martinez she later returned with her father to Germany. Here she took a position with the east German Ministry of State Security. It was there the East German secret service spotted her and approached her to become one of their agents.

She was completely trained in Soviet style espionage and in the spring of 1959 given her first major assignment. She was to meet Che Guevara who was coming to East Berlin to negotiate a loan for his government. With her South American background and language skills she was perfect for the assignment.

The loan took several weeks. During this time their friendship blossomed into love. Guevara, however, now had to return to Cuba at the conclusion of his mission.

Desiring to keep close tabs on him Laura was sent to Cuba where, thanks to Guevara's influence, she got a job with the University of Havana. During this time she was constantly sending back reports to her Soviet bosses, keeping them apprised of just what was going on •

Five years later, in 1964, she reported to the KGB Guevara was being transferred to Bolivia to spread his brand of Marxism. Somewhat concerned the KGB ordered her to follow him. Lacking Bolivian citizenship she promptly obeyed her party and married a Bolivian, Antonio Martinez. Following that she dumped him. She took a new name—Tania. She found a way to provide Guevara with forged documents proclaiming him to be an American sociologist engaged in research.

In a few months Guevara had built a small underground army. This did not please the KGB who feared he was not only becoming too powerful but also teaching a brand of Marxism harmful to Russia. The KGB asserted its muscle and ordered Tania to betray him.

In March 1967 she did just that telling the Bolivian General Juan Torres of his whereabouts. It resulted in Guevera's capture and eventual assassination by a Bolivian sergeant.

Tania was not heard from again. It is assumed she died in the firefight where he was finally captured.

XCI
Bracha Fuld

She fought the Nazis, then she fought the British in Israel's struggle for independence. On March 26, 1946, at the age of 29, Bracha Fuld fell in battle.

Her life began in luxury in Berlin. A large mansion, complete with servants, was home to Bracha, her sister, Petra, and her parents. Her father was a successful industrialist. When Hitler came into power the Fuld family, all good Germans, shuddered at the sight of the goose stepping Nazis whose goals were all too evident.

She pleaded with her parents to leave Germany since they, all Jews, were not wanted and, in fact, in grave danger.

Her father refused, saying he had fought honorably in World War I and no harm would come to them.

Their world came to an end with the Nazi order effective Nov. 9, 1938 to burn all synagogues and deport and liquidate all Jews. Her mother got Petra into America and herself and Bracha into England. Her father remained behind. A few weeks later they were told her father had committed suicide.

Bracha fell in love with England. Free of worry over Nazism she studied and enjoyed the country and its freedom. But her mother faced the problem of a divided family and no means of support since her husband was now dead.

Over Bracha's protests she and her mother emigrated to the new land, Palestine. Bracha was truly an outsider. She did not speak Hebrew as did the other children. She had no knowledge of Zionism or the history of this new land.

In addition there was a decided division between the European Jewish children and the 'sabras'. These were the Jewish children born in Palestine who learned Hebrew first, then English and Arabic.

Bracha, a bright child, failed in school. Her teacher said of her, "she is arrogant, conceited, isolated and just plain difficult".

Her teacher took an interest in this difficult child and taught her Ivrith, the new language. In addition she joined Habonim, a youth group.

When Germany invaded Poland in Sept. 1939 Bracha refused to speak German any more.

The war presented Britain with a problem. They wanted the support of the Jews but did not want them to be armed and taught how to fight. They knew the problem of an independent Jewish state would follow the end of the war.

Finally in desperation they agreed to work with the Jewish defense group, Haganah. The Haganah worked with primitive weapons lacking guns and ammunition. They engaged in espionage by living as Arabs among the Germans and bringing back information. Out of the Haganah came the Palmach which continued training after the Nazi defeat.

Bracha was now 17. She told her mother she had been training with the Palmach and wanted her permission to join. Her mother blanched knowing of the extreme danger that awaited these young people.

Knowing her headstrong daughter would simply run away, her mother gave in. Possibly she secretly agreed with her wishes.

Romance entered the picture. Bracha met a young man appropriately named Gideon. While the attraction was strong between them the goal of a free Israel took precedence. They walked and talked but made no permanent plans.

Eventually Gideon was arrested and put in prison for treason by the British. Bracha visited him as often as possible (every two months) and even her mother got into the act by baking him goods containing special messages.

It was during one of these visits Bracha met another man with whom she fell in love. But he was quite different. He was Shelby, a British officer—an enemy.

He began by asking her what she thought of prison conditions. His questions portrayed a sensitive man who did not hate the Jews but was merely bound to do his duty.

The two became close and he asked her to marry him. It was dangerous for them to be out—the British would have problems of his being with a Jew and her people would likewise condemn her for associating with him.

Torn with guilt over her association with him and Gideon in prison she asked him to delay any marriage plans till the warfare was settled.

In this period of discussions between them he revealed he sided with the Jews and their wishes as did the rest of the world. Finally he agreed to help the Haganah, risking his own career and, possibly his life.

In the Valley of Sharon, a Jewish stronghold, Bracha was leading a group in gymnastics on the dining hall floor when the British raided them. Bracha was secretly training over 300 recruits there and the British got word of their activity.

Not a word was exchanged between the British and the Jews as the soldiers conducted their raid looking for weapons.

Finding nothing the British left. As soon as they were out of sight the Jews tore up the dining hall floor where they had hidden their weapons. A timely tip by Shelby had forewarned them.

The fighting and killing intensified. No British soldier was safe alone. Jews were arrested, beaten and imprisoned.

In March 1946 word came that a ship was to land illegally bearing more refugees. One thousand Haganah activists were alerted. On the night of the ships arrival the lights went out, streets were blocked by trucks and cars and the city became tense.

Bracha commanded a roadblock in a ramshackle house with eight boys. They were up against British troops and tanks. A British patrol came upon them and, not knowing their strength, returned for reinforcements. During this time a runner came up to tell her the awaited ship had been captured by the British and they were to return.

Bracha said it was not an official order and decided to hold her ground until properly relieved. She told the boys with her they were free to leave. Four of them did.

When the British returned a fierce firefight developed. She was hit in the chest and told the others to run for it—she would fight as long as she could.

Though mortally wounded she survived long enough to be questioned briefly by the British. She answered nothing, then died. When the British searched her home they found nothing that would incriminate Shelby. Her mother had destroyed all his letters.

More Jews arrived later on a ship named BRACHA FULD. Many of them were taken to see the ramshackle hut where she had held her position and was killed.

CHAPTER 11

▼

XCII
Hilda X Aka Hilda Brandt Aka ???

She was a woman whose name was never known although she had an extremely high profile in atomic spy circles. She was closely associated with atom spy, Dr. Klaus Emil Julius Fuchs. The name 'Brandt' was given her by the Communist Party. It means 'fire' in German. She also was called Heiss, Warm and Kalt, all German names for various temperatures.

She and Fuchs met at Kiel University in the early 1930s. They came together at a Communist party function where he was a cell leader of Party functionaries. She was new and immediately fell for him, following him with stars in her eyes.

They passed out handbills, attended public rallies, wrote letters to editors. They were fueled not only by their belief in the solidarity of the working class but their hatred of the Nazi system and its evils. Fuchs had a special reason to hate the Nazis. One of his sisters suffered a nervous breakdown. Another jumped under a train to her death. His father was deported to a concentration camp.

Fuchs instructed her daily and she grew more and more dedicated to the Communist cause.

The two knew they must leave Germany. Preparations were carefully made. She went to England. He got to France and remained there for a while, then joined her. He studied at Bristol University.

England greatly appealed to him and he lost himself in studies. He put her and his pursuit of Communism on hold to her chagrin. She also worried he seemed to like the British women. Finally she left him telling him his capitalist friends in Britain would one day betray him.

Her next move was to become a courier for the Communists. She traveled around the continent. Fuchs went to Edinburgh University where he received his degree as a doctor of science in 1938. His papers on nuclear and atomic physics had brought him great prominence and the praise of the scientific community.

Hilda was organizing spy rings in Poland, Czechoslovakia, Scandinavia and even inside Germany. The two drifted further apart and stopped writing each other.

She had been instructed by the Party to drop him as he had done with the Communist cause. Obedient to the party, she did so. When Hitler invaded Poland Fuchs suddenly became an enemy alien in British eyes. He was told to prepare for deportation to Canada immediately.

Alone in his hut in Canada Hilda's words about being betrayed one day by the British came back to haunt him. He wondered where she was and longed to see her again.

In perfect timing a letter from her arrived telling him she was in the U.S. and wondered about him. Did he need money?

With communication restored Hilda brought him back into the Communist line and he rededicated himself to that cause.

His brilliance in atomic research was not overlooked by America, desperate to develop the atom bomb. In 1941 he was released from internment and brought to America to work in that field.

Hilda had left by now. No one knew for sure where she was. Even though his Communist background was known it was overshadowed by the desire to get his knowledge and develop that special weapon.

They did not meet again until after the war. By then he had become a member of the Soviet Secret Service and Russia's top atom spy. The man who inducted him had been sent by Hilda.

They spent the night making love and professing their dedication to one another. The next day was a rainy Sunday.

Hilda watched history in the making as Fuchs headed toward Trafalgar Square. Another man joined him briefly. Fuchs handed him an envelope and continued on his way. He headed down a nearby subway and disappeared.

The envelope saved Russia ten years of atomic research. At his trial Fuchs stated he had a split personality. One was good, the other evil. He now hated Communism and knew it was bad for mankind.

Rumors placed Hilda in various places since his trial but no one knows for sure where she is. She faults herself for his problems saying she should have let him be just the scientist he was and not getting him involved as a Soviet secret agent.

XCIII
Nora Korzhenko

In the Vatican the Holy Father received a woman seeking removal of a tremendous burden that troubled her soul.

The year was 1950. The woman was Nora Korzhenko, a high-level Russian spy. With her were her three children.

"I was a Russian spy. I want to confess and I want to fall before the Holy Fathers' feet", she said.

She had not entered the field of espionage freely. It was really a matter of doing so or facing death.

Her father was Wassil Korzhenko, a member of the general staff of the Soviet Revolution in 1917. He was in charge of controlling foreign diplomats in Russia. As such he was chief of the secret police in Leningrad and organized his own spy network. Along with Beria he was one of the most hated men in Russia.

His luck ran out in 1939. Stalin had just signed his non-aggression pact with Hitler. Stalin decided it was time to purge the 'old guard'. Korzhenko was shot.

Nora, born in 1919, was told she could either become a spy or join her father in death. It helped her make up her mind. With her mother dead and her stepmother deported Nora was actually an outcast.

All of her 20 years had been spent under Communism. It was all she knew. Now she was forced into the OGPU and became a Mozhno girl. Her job was to spy on foreign diplomats. The OGPU ordered her to become the mistress of various foreign diplomats.

With the threat of deportation to Siberia looming she found it too much. She confided her situation to a Rumanian diplomat. He gave her assistance by providing simple information she could pass on to the OGPU making her look good.

Her next assignment was the secretary of the British Naval Attache, John Murray. Knowing the caliber of the Mozhno women he asked her to get out. Her supervisors at OGPU told her to either produce or face immediate deportation.

Desperate, she went back to Murray and confided in him. A tough decision faced Murray. While he suspected a typical Communist trick he also saw a frightened woman and recognized a definite possibility of OGPU blackmail against her. He decided he would gamble and help her although protecting his own flanks.

Her relief turned to panic when Murray was suddenly ordered to return to his home.

Going for broke she fled and headed for the place where she felt he could be found. She had completely broken with her country of birth.

Her trip took her through icy roads in the Arctic, blizzards and bluffing her way through the OGPU guards who stopped her constantly. Miraculously she found his ship and rejoined Murray just before he sailed.

He married her. They live in London with their three children.

XCIV
Elizabeth Bentley

The well-dressed woman, in her thirties, sat in her comfortable New York apartment pondering a terrible dilemma. In her hand was an envelope containing $2,000 in new $20 bills. It had just been given to her by a Communist courier as a reward for outstanding work she had done over the years in infiltrating the American government. It was 1945.

Elizabeth Bentley had been a Communist spy since 1933 and was thoroughly knowledgeable in their beliefs and organization. She had been responsible for Communist spies at all levels and in most departments of the U.S. government. She personally met with at least twenty pro-Communist American government workers weekly in all departments of the War Production Board and the Treasury Department. Included were those working in the Army, Air Force and Patent office. In actuality she said she had contacts with all departments except the Navy and the FBI. She even told of contacts within the Atomic Energy Commission.

She was a graduate of Vassar and Columbia where her cells had discovered the Americans had broken the Soviet code. They were advised of this and immediately changed their codes.

In 1933, after graduating from Vassar, she went to Italy where she became a Communist. She reported the Fascism she saw was so horrible she was drawn to the Communist propaganda.

Back in America at Columbia University she met Yasha Golos, a Communist courier, and became his common law wife.

At various meeting places she was passed information on all kinds of secret plans. These were promptly given the Soviets.

She shocked grand juries with testimony that she received all types of highly sensitive information on the OSS, secret negotiations in the Balkans and even that they knew of the D-Day plans and dates before they happened. She personally knew and met with Eleanor Roosevelt and had contact with one of the President's key men. Information from the White House was in Russian hands within twenty-four hours.

Her testimony ruined careers and imprisoned many Americans who had betrayed their country. Some had unwittingly given her information.

And now, sitting alone with the $2,000 in hand, Elizabeth Bentley repented. She realized the enormity of her crime and was repulsed by it all.

The next morning she appeared at the desk of the FBI Chief in Foley Square, New York, and said she wanted to confess. She laid the $2,000 on the table and began her long, sordid tale.

She was hated and labeled a Judas by those she named. They claimed she was lying to protect her own skin. No one was ever able to prove she had lied.

Her government believed her when she said, "It was my good old New England conscience that led me to quit the Communist underground and tell Federal authorities all I knew."

She provided the greatest in depth expose ever known into the duplicity and depth of Communist espionage.

XCV
Elfriede Eisler Aka Ruth Fischer

She emerged from the ghettos of Vienna near the beginning of the 20th century. Her father was a brilliant but starving intellectual who had produced thirty philosophical works. Her father, Dr· Rudolph Eisler, spent up to sixteen hours a day to finish one of his edifying works. Sadly it did not pay rent or for food or clothing and the children suffered.

She and her brothers, Hanns and Gerhart spent an unhappy childhood dreaming of the things other children's parents were able to provide. One brother was content to follow a musical career. The other went into the army in 1917 and fought against the Allies. While she studied economics and history her mind and heart were captured by the radical student movement seeking an end to warfare and butchery. It was the end of World War I and Europe was in upheaval.

The Communists sent emissaries into Austria seeking new members. The first cardholder was a woman named Ruth Fischer who was actually Elfriede Eisler. Also joining but not for totally idealistic purposes, were her two brothers. The climate in Austria was not favorable to Communism and she was ordered to the more revolutionary prone areas. These included Bavaria and Hungary. Then she was sent to Berlin which was ready for her. She was a gifted speaker and was intelligent as well as good looking. She flourished and brought many into the party.

In 1921 she was elected to the post of chairman of the Berlin Communist party even though not a German citizen. The next year she attended the fourth Congress of the Communist International in Moscow.

There she met Lenin, Trotsky and Stalin. All of them expressed admiration for her work. She said Germany was ready for revolution and proposed they begin at once. It was Lenin who put the brakes on saying, "We can't export Communism from Russia; all countries have to find their own form of Communism". Nevertheless one of the German communist members sought the confrontation and ran into the new Nazi party that defeated it. The threat of a Red Germany faded.

She met a fellow worker, Arcadi Maslow, and married him. In the meantime she had been elected to the Reichstag, the German Parliament. She sat to the far left and was derided as a troublemaker who 'sneers and snarls', interrupting with cries of 'pfui'. She sat in the Reichstag until 1928. Over this period she met with Stalin and Tito several times. Stalin admired her as a strong woman but feared her as being too strong and he had no use for a woman who wouldn't take orders. Also he was upset she did not consider Russia came first....Russian communists must rule the German party. She refused and he placed her under house arrest.

Knowing others were being purged she felt the noose tightening around her neck. Stalin, tired from his last battle with Trotsky before his exile, left on a long vacation.

Seizing the opportunity she called on friends still loyal to her and was able to leave Russia after feigning sickness at a meeting. She returned to Germany where she was still a member of the Reichstag. In the middle of the Stalin-Lenin-Trotsky power struggle she and others split. Her brother backed Stalin, she, Lenin.

Convinced she was the true Communist she broke and in 1929 revealed her brother had been sent underground in China. She exposed the secret dealings between the Gestapo and Russia's G.P.U. to wreck democracy in Germany.

In 1939 she and her husband fled to Cuba where they kept up the fight. He was a superb investigator and found out and exposed many details of Communist skullduggery.

With Stalin firmly entrenched she became more and more violent in her attacks on him. The final blow came when her husband collapsed on a street in Havana and died. He had been poisoned by the same people who had murdered Trotsky.

She came to America and told all she knew. She said her brother Gerhart was in America and gave his new name. She informed them her brother Hanns wrote songs for the Communist International and was in Hollywood. The Rockefeller Foundation had given him a $20,000 grant for research in modern music.

The split between brother and sister was deep and unforgiving. Brother Gerhart stated, "I would like to kill her", and so would many others.

She revealed the names of hundreds of Communists and exposed their network that many found hard to believe existed. Even Eleanor Roosevelt had been taken in by brother Gerhart.

She led the anti-Communist forces with all the strength, cunning and vigor she had ever used in the days when she promoted their world-wide plan for domination.

XCVI
Ethel Rosenberg

The case of Ethel Rosenberg and her husband, Julius, will always be divisive and debatable. They were instrumental in advancing the Russian atom bomb by many years with the information they provided.

As the children of Jewish immigrants some felt it was anti-Semitism that brought them the death penalty. Others were just against the death penalty in any event. But many more felt they deserved their sentence because their espionage had been during wartime.

They were recruited as spies by Anatoli Yakovlev who was the New York KGB officer. Ethel was the stronger of the two. Her brother, David Greenglass, was a machinist for the Manhattan Project. He gave her rough drawings of the detonating device for the atomic bomb in January 1945. The detonating of the bomb had been a major problem for the Manhattan Project for many months. The drawings were passed on to the Russians and four years later they exploded their first atomic bomb.

When the investigation finally revealed the guilty parties, Greenglass confessed and implicated the others. He received a fifteen year sentence. Two others in the ring received similar sentences.

The Rosenbergs, however, pleaded not guilty and went to trial. They were found guilty and given the death penalty. Leaders worldwide, as well as many Americans, pleaded for a prison sentence instead of death. They pointed out others in the ring had been given only prison terms.

President Eisenhower held firm. He said while it was reprehensible to execute a woman who had children it would send a message if it was not done. The Russians, he felt, would realize our reluctance to execute a woman and simply switch to recruiting women.

The sentencing judge, Irving Kaufman, said not only had they provided the bomb to Russia but that act had encouraged the Communist Korean aggression resulting in thousands of casualties. They were executed in 1953.

Vasilli Metrokhin, Chief of Russia's KGB, in his book, THE SWORD AND THE SHIELD, said the Rosenberg's produced so many documents Russia feared America was sending false information. The Rosenberg's code names were Ultra and Liberal in KGB records.

XCVII
Myra X

She had once been an attractive woman but had lost it all in the Nazi concentration camp at Belsen where American troops freed her. We don't know her full name. She came from the camp a mad woman. Mad in both senses of that word. The inhumane treatment of her and her fellow Jews pushed her over the brink.

After her release she needed psychiatric treatment which she never got. No one wanted her. All borders were closed. She had one alternative only...that of becoming an immigrant to the new nation of Israel. She took it.

In her opinion all British were to be treated like Nazis and all Arabs liquidated. It was her desire to die in open warfare, fighting for all she believed in.

In Israel she asked for the most hazardous jobs but even the most violent Jewish organizations recognized her problems and refused her. Social workers put her in an institution for treatment but she escaped.

The period was now that of the new nation, Israel, being carved out of territory the Arabs considered theirs alone. The new United Nations was trying to bring a peaceful solution to these longtime enemies.

The man foremost in the news was Sweden's Count Folke Bernadotte. He had been heavily involved in the Jewish problem and was one of the first to enter the grisly concentration camps right after the Nazi defeat. He had spent countless days trying to help the Jews escape Hitler's wrath.

In 1944 Bernadotte had had several meetings with hated Gestapo Chief Heinrich Himmler in an attempt to end the war. This, to the distorted mind of Myra X, was tantamount to a conspiracy against the Jews by both men and since she could not kill Himmler, Bernadotte would have to do.

At a Red Cross convention in Stockholm Bernadotte was warned by the Swedish Jewish community that a mad woman, Myra X, might try to assassinate him. The guard was doubled and Bernadotte laughed it off.

Several weeks later he left for Palestine in hopes he could mediate peace between the Arabs and Jews. One of the proposals would have put the Wailing Wall in Arab hands. The British considered it proper but both Jews and Arabs fought it.

On September 17, 1948 his white peace plane flew low over the Judean hills. The plane had been warned by radio that they would be fired on if they landed at the

Kalandia airport. Bernadotte dismissed it and they landed with no problem.

A propaganda barrage led by Myra X greeted the UN party and Bernadotte was warned to go back to Stockholm. He ignored it.

In his Red Cross uniform he first went to the suburbs of Ramallah outside the city of Jerusalelm. Then he went on into Jerusalem. As his car approached Mount Scopus it was fired on from the hills. His running-board was hit and a tire was punctured. When the tire was changed the small caravan continued.

It went to the Vale of Kidron which housed the Red Cross and United Nations staff. When they left the group was divided into three cars. The first two bore the Red Cross flag. The third had the blue and white United Nations' flag.

Bernadotte's car had a U.S. officer in the front. In the back with Bernadotte was a French observer and a Swedish General.

The three cars had passed several road blocks but were stopped at the foot of the Hill of Evil where Satan allegedly tempted Jesus. A party of five men and one woman stopped them. They were armed with Sten guns.

Thinking it simply another traffic check the cars stopped. As they did so the people opened fire. One stuck a gun through the window of the Bernadotte car and fired. It killed the French observer immediately. Bernadotte's chest was raked by bullets. The assassins fled.

Bernadotte was still alive, but barely. They drove as quickly as possible to the Hadassah hospital but he was dead on arrival.

The world was outraged. Israel sent its deepest apologies to Countess Bernadotte and the Swedish government.

The carefully planned plot was thorough in its knowledge of the itinerary and timing of the UN visit. Israeli courts stated the assassins were trained men and women. What Myra had learned in the concentration camp had well prepared her. The court detailed the following points:

(a) there was a clear decision to assassinate the Count and a detailed plan for its implementation;

(b)

(c) a complex espionage network that could keep track of his time and thereby set their own schedule for the attack;

(d)

(e) people experienced in this type of activity and trained for it;

(f)

(g) the appropriate arms and equipment to carry it out;

(h)

(i) an experienced commander who would be responsible.

(j)

The assassins escaped by plane and disappeared into Czechoslovakia where they were never heard of again. Who knows what else Myra X might have dreamed up— or even accomplished.

XCVIII
Grandma

She was one of the shrewdest investigators America had known. A respectable bespectacled woman in her sixties she had the patience and cunning to dig deep into the most complex cases. Her name cannot be divulged even to this date although she was active prior to World War two along with her husband.

They were quite active in the young Communist movement. Her husband was alleged to be the chief OGPU agent in America. Grandma believed Russia was the answer to all problems and could bring everlasting peace, joy and happiness to mankind.

Then the day came when her world collapsed. She learned her husband had been embezzling funds and squandering them on Russian dancers, students and couriers.

During this time she was approached by a secret agent who felt she was ripe to desert the movement along with her husband. He read the script correctly.

She opened the doors of Communist conspiracy wide to the FBI and for years was an open conduit of their operations. She was able to tell the American government of Politburo happenings almost immediately after they were held.

Her revenge against her husband was to totally betray the Communist movement which she did with great dispatch. He died during WWII and she lost her pipeline into Communism.

But now there was no need to carry on her deception and she moved into the FBI offices to the consternation of her Communist colleagues.

Her work has been so secret even her grandchildren know nothing about her and simply say her many trips are merely vacations. Her mission was to run down others who had been involved with Hilda X and Claude Fuchs, now convicted spies. Fuchs had alluded to others who were involved and the FBI wanted to know who else had betrayed America.

Her instructions were to first find the women he had been involved with. She was given an open budget and told to take as much time as she deemed necessary.

She went to the University at Kiel and asked questions. She examined letters sent and received by Fuchs while he was in Canada. She interviewed Fuchs who cooperated. He told her one man who had sold secrets had worked at a plant in Syracuse. His name was Alfred Dean Slack. Grandma talked to his first wife, then his second. The facts were confirmed and Slack was convicted for espionage.

He had innocently fallen into the Soviet trap. At the time we were friendly with Russia he was instructed to give them some information which he did. Other reports followed and he felt he was merely helping a developing society that would truly be a workers paradise. He saw our own depression and what it had done to America and fell prey to the capitalist oppression theory.

Slowly he fell deeper into the trap and when he was transferred to Oak Ridge he was pestered again and again for some new explosive formulas. He refused. His contact advised he had better cooperate or he would be exposed to the FBI and lose his job and reputation.

He caved and in 1943 gave the information. At his trial and conviction he appeared to have aged many years. He was haggard and downcast.

Grandma sat silently in the courtroom. No one would have dreamed this elderly lady had been the one gathering evidence to convict him.

She was next on the trail of another unknown figure known only as comrade Henry Fuchs and Slack both described him as dark, thin faced with a sad look below a high forehead. He talked in fast, clipped fashion and was always well dressed. In time the man proved to be Harry Gold, also under observation for leftist leanings.

The evidence was sufficient for his conviction and once again Grandma sat silently in the courtroom, her hands folded over her purse.

On December 5, 1950, Gold confessed to his misdeeds in court. He said, "There is a puny inadequacy about any words telling how deep and horrible is my remorse...most certainly this could never happen in the Soviet Union or in any of the countries dominated by it."

He was sentenced to thirty years.

Further convictions did follow.

POSTLUDE

What happens when former spies go back to their normal lives? Do they easily slip back into regular roles or are their lives forever changed—for the better or worse?

Some years ago at an OSS reunion in Las Vegas I noticed some of those I had served with were not at the gambling tables or slot machines. When I asked if they didn't gamble their reply was simply they did not because they felt they had already used up all of their luck.

It was a boast of the OSS veterans that none if its people were known to have used their 'talents' for personal gain once they had left their espionage roles. Many became known in the judicial system, in politics, entertainment and industry.

The women seemed less inclined to talk about their roles. Some of them would not even discuss those days they walked the thin line. The cruel games go on out of necessity for national security—and now industrial security also.

Our lethal ladies, together with their brothers, will continue playing their vital role in these ongoing battles.

BIBLIOGRAPHY

Ameringer, Charles D., U.S. FOREIGN INTELLI-
GENCE, New York 1990

Bower, Donald E., SEX EXPIONAGE, New York, 1990

Callwood, June, EMMA: CANADA'S UNLIKELY SPY,
New York 1985

Casey, Bill, THE SECRET WAR AGAINST GERMANY,
WASHINGTON D.C. 1978

Corson, Wm. R. THE ARMIES OF IGNORANCE, New
York 1977

Craft of Intelligence, The, ALLEN DULLER, New York
1963

Dulles, Alien W., THE CRAFT OF INTELLIGENCE,
New York 1963

Files, Yvonne, THE QUEST FOR FREEDOM, Santa
Barbara 1988

Ford, Corey, DONOVAN OF OSS, Boston 1970

Hall, Richard, PATRIOTS IN DISGUISE, New York 1993

Haswell, Jock, SPIES AND SPYMAASTERS, London 1977

Horrocks, Wm., IN THEIR OWN WORDS, ONTARIO
1993

Hyde, Montgomery, SECRET INTELLIGENCE AGENT, New York 1983

Hymoff, Edward, THE OSS IN WORLD WAR II, New York 1986

Icardo, Also, AMERICAN MASTER SPY, New York, 1956

Kobler, John, HE RUNS A PRIVATE OSS, Saturday Evening Post 1955

Lovell, Mary S., CAST NO SHADOW, New York 1992

Lovell, Stanley, OF SPIES AND STRATAGEMS, New Jersey 1963

McIntosh, Elizabeth, (Betty) SISTERHOOD OF SPIES Annapolis 1998

THE ROLE OF WOMEN IN INTELLIGENCE, Monographs from the Assoc. of Former Intelligence Officers, Virginia, 1989

Melchoir, Ib, CASE BY CASE, Novata, CA 1993

MILITARY INTELLIGENCE, ITS HEROES AND LEGENDS, U.S. Army

Miller, Marion, MY DARK DAYS AS A COUNTERSPY, Readers Digest 1959

Miller, Nathan, SPYING FOR AMERICA, New York 1989

Mitrohkin, 'Vasili THE SWORD AND SHIELD New York 1999

Moon, Tom and Eifler, THE DEADLIEST COLONEL, New York 1975

Moon, Tom, THIS GRIM AND SAVAGE GAME, Los Angeles 1992

Morgan, Dr. William, THE OSS AND I, New York 1957

Nicolson, Harold, THE WAR YEARS, 1967

Palmer, Raymond, THE ENCYCLOPEDIA OF ESPIONAGE, London 1977

Persico, Joseph E., PIERCING THE REICH, New York 1979

Roosevelt, Kermit, WAR REPORT OF THE OSS, Volumes I and II New York 1975

Romanones, Countess Aline, THE SPY WORE RED, New York 1987

Romanones, Countess Aline, THE SPY WENT DANC-ING, New York 1988

Singer, Kurt, THE WORLD'S 30 GREATEST WOMEN SPIES, New York 1951

Smith, R. Harris, OSS, Berkeley, 1972

Stern, Philip Van Doren, SECRET MISSIONS OF THE CIVIL WAR, Chicago 1959

Thayer, George, THE WAR BUSINESS, New York 1969

THE SUPER SPIES, New York 1969

Time-Life Books, THE SECRET WAR, New York 1980

Tully, Andrew, CIA THE INSIDE STORY, New York 1962

ROSTER

Rahab	II
Richer, Martha (the Lark)	XXVII
Romer, Joy	LXIV
Rosenberg, Ethel	XCVI
Rousseau, Jeanne	LXI
Rowden, Diana	LX
Sansom, Odette	LVIII
Schragmuller, Dr. Elsbeth	XXI
Sergueiev, Lily	LXXIV
Severens, Marjorie	XXXIX
Shi Pei Pu	LXXXV
Shippen, Peggy	V
Skarbek, Countess (Granville)	LXXVIII
Smedley, Agnes	XLIV
Switz, Marjorie	LXXVII
Szabo, Violette	LVII
Tannous, Rima	LXXXVI
Taylor, Peggy	XXXVI
Thompson, Sarah	XVII
Toguri, Iva	LXXXI
Tubman, Harriett	XII
Van Lew, Elizabeth (Crazy Bet)	VIII
Velazquez, Loreta Vera	XIII
Vera (Italian woman)	LXXVI
Walker, Dr. Mary Edwards	XVIII
Wolkoff, Anne	LII
Wright, Patience Mehitabel Lovell	VI
Wright, Rebecca	XV